CW01276683

Speak Japanese!

日本人がよく使う
日本語会話
オノマトペ基本表現180

ぎおんご・ぎたいご

180 Basic Onomatopoeia (Giongo-Gitaigo) Expressions Used by Native Japanese Speakers in Regular Conversation

清ルミ 著
Sei Rumi

Jリサーチ出版

はじめに
Foreword

日本語会話では、オノマトペは非常によく使われています。オノマトペを知らないと、日本語として自然な表現にはなりませんし、会話そのものが成り立ちません。

それほど大切な役割を担うオノマトペですが、残念なことに日本語学習においては教科書に登場する頻度は高くなく、断片的に扱われることが多いのが現状です。

そこで、本書は、言いたいことを的確に伝えるために重要なオノマトペにスポットライトを当て、基本的な語だけを厳選して取り上げました。全体を４つの大きなパート（「動詞と一緒に使う」「動作や変化の特徴を表す」「ものの状態を表す・強調する」「心の状態を表す」）に分け、さらに使いやすいようにテーマや特徴から小さく分類しました。そして、一つ一つの語を運用面から丁寧に解説しました。解説の日本語レベルはＮ３程度です。ニュアンスを把握していただきやすいよう効果的なイラストも入れ、日本人の使用頻度が高い会話例を出しました。付属の収録音声も、ニュアンスをより一層理解するのに役立てていただけると思います。

オノマトペを学んで、より自然な日本語を身につけてください。

清ルミ

Onomatopoeic expressions are used very often in Japanese conversations. It isn't possible to express yourself naturally in Japanese without knowing onomatopoeias, nor can proper conversations be had at all.

While onomatopoeias play such a vital role in Japanese, they unfortunately appear infrequently in Japanese learning textbooks, and when they do, they often appear in fragmentary ways.

That is why this book shines a spotlight on onomatopoeias that are important to accurately conveying what you want to say, carefully selecting only the most fundamental terms. It consists of four major parts, onomatopoeias used together with verbs, ones that express what is notable about an action or change, ones that express or highlight the state of something, and ones that express a mental or emotional state. From there, terms are sorted into more narrow classifications based on theme or characteristic in order to make this book even easier to use. Each term also has a thorough explanation regarding how it is used, written at around the JLPT N3 level. Effective illustrations that make it easier for you to understand the nuances of each term are included as well, as are conversation examples of situations where Japanese people would frequently use the term. The attached voice recordings should also help you to get an even stronger understanding of the nuances of each term.

We hope you become able to use Japanese in an even more natural way by learning onomatopoeias.

Rumi Sei

目次（もくじ）
Table of Contents

この本の使い方
How to Use this Book

この本で取り上げたオノマトペは、全部で 180 語あります。

There are 180 onomatopoeias featured in this book.

取り上げたオノマトペは大きく４つのパートに分け、さらにペアや小さなグループに分けています。

It is split into 4 large sections that are then further divided into pairs and smaller groups.

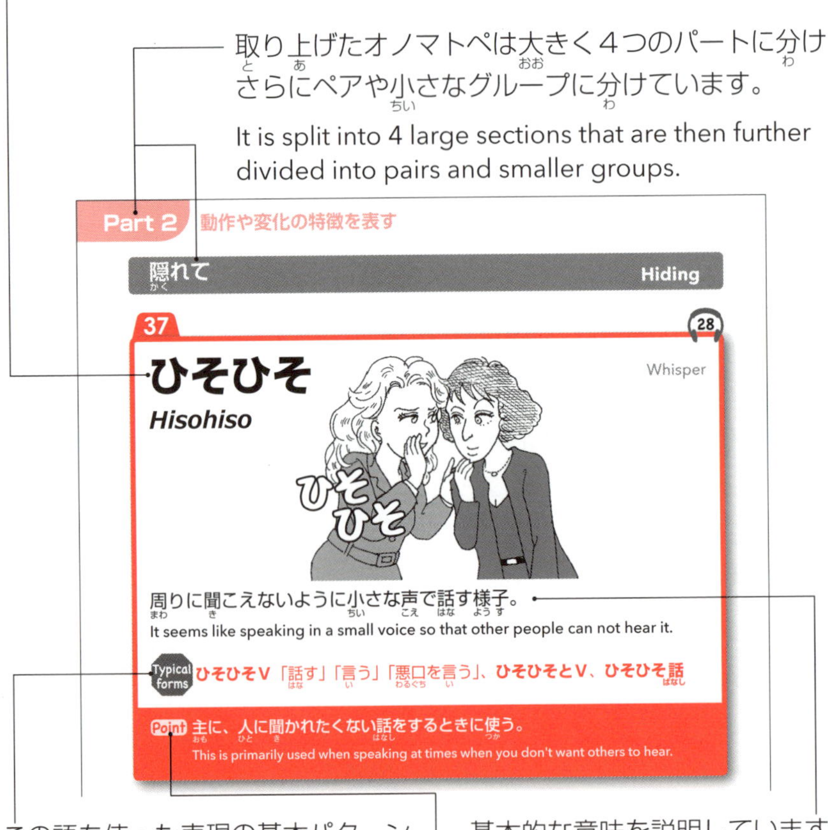

この語を使った表現の基本パターンを示しています。

Basic expression patterns that use this phrase are given.

基本的な意味を説明しています。

The basic meaning of the term are explained.

意味や使う場面を理解するポイントを示しています。

Points to help you better understand the term's meaning and the situation in which it is used are given.

会話またはモノローグの例を２つ紹介しています。
Two examples of dialogues or monologues are introduced.

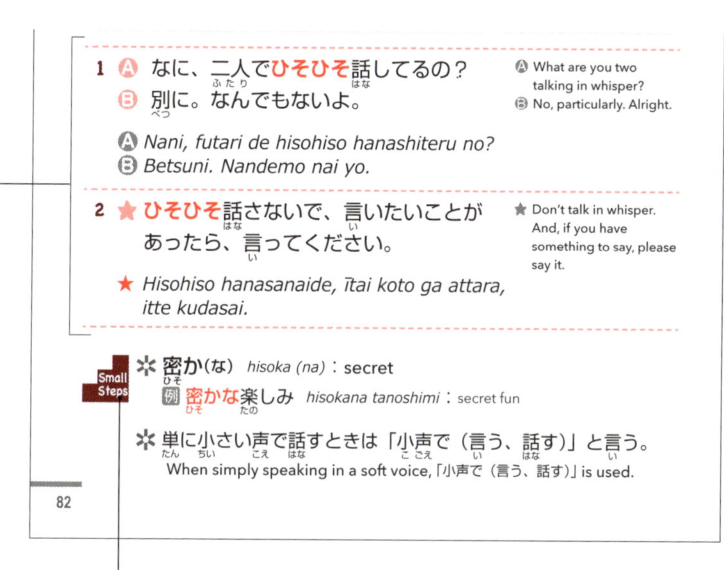

1 Ⓐ なに、二人でひそひそ話してるの？
Ⓑ 別に。なんでもないよ。

Ⓐ Nani, futari de hisohiso hanashiteru no?
Ⓑ Betsuni. Nandemo nai yo.

Ⓐ What are you two talking in whisper?
Ⓑ No, particularly. Alright.

2 ★ ひそひそ話さないで、言いたいことがあったら、言ってください。

★ Hisohiso hanasanaide, ītai koto ga attara, itte kudasai.

★ Don't talk in whisper. And, if you have something to say, please say it.

Small Steps

✲ 密か(な) hisoka (na)：secret
例 密かな楽しみ hisokana tanoshimi：secret fun

✲ 単に小さい声で話すときは「小声で（言う、話す）」と言う。
When simply speaking in a soft voice,「小声で（言う、話す）」is used.

82

関連する表現などを取り上げ、説明しています。
Related expressions and more are introduced and explained.

音声ダウンロードの案内は、本の一番後ろの部分にあります。
Information on how to download voice information can be found in the back of this book.

CDの使い方
How to Use the CD

付属CDには、各ユニットで紹介されている例文が収録されています（日本語のみ）。

The attached CD includes recordings of example sentences introduced in them (in Japanese only).

❶まず最初に、会話文をざっと読んでみましょう。会話が行われている場面をイメージしながら、意味を理解しましょう。

❷次に、本を見ながらCDを聴きましょう。話している人がどんな気持ちか、想像しながら聞いてください。また、アクセントやイントネーションなど、音のニュアンスにも注意しながら、その表現がどのように使われるか、確認しましょう。

❸本を見ながら、CDの音をまねるように、声に出して読んでみましょう。

❹本を見ないで聴いて、意味を理解しましょう。また、CDの音を追いかけるように口に出して言ってみましょう。

1: Begin by quickly reading over the conversation. Imagine the scene in which the conversation is taking place and understand what is being said.

2: Next, take a look at the book while listening to the CD. Imagine how the speakers feel as you hear them talk. As you confirm how each expression is used, also pay attention to details in how the words are being spoken, such as the speaker's accent and intonation.

3: Look at the book and read aloud the conversations while imitating the speakers in the CD.

4: Listen to the CD without looking at the book and understand what is being said. Also try repeating after the CD as you listen to it.

序章◆日本語会話に欠かせないオノマトペ

Introduction◆Onomatopoeias, an Essential Part of Japanese Conversations

ニュアンスが伝わる、感情が伝わる

日本語では、日常の会話でも文章でも、オノマトペが非常によく使われます。さまざまな場面で、見たもの感じたもの、心に思ったことなどが表現でき、それが相手にストレートに伝わるからです。

「彼女はにっこりと笑った。彼女の目がキラキラしていて、僕はドキドキしてしまった」。このような文を読めば、「彼女」が上品な美しい人で、「僕」は「彼女」に恋をしているということがすぐわかります。このように、どんな人がどのような状況で何をしているか、長々と言葉で説明しなくても、ニュアンスを正確に伝えるのが、オノマトペです。リズミカルで感情が素直に伝わり、親しみやすいのです。

さまざまな分野、場面で使われる

日本語のオノマトペの数は、ヨーロッパ言語や中国語の３～５倍で、１万語以上あると言われています。欧米では、オノマトペは主に子供が使うもので、大人が使うと幼稚で教養がないという印象を与えるようです。しかし、日本語では、医療、スポーツ、美容、広告、漫画など、あらゆる分野で効果的に使われ、認知科学の研究分野でも注目を浴びています。オノマトペが商品名に用いられ、ヒットしたものもたくさんあります。お菓子では「ガリガリ君」「プッチンプリン」、家庭用品では「ゴキブリホイホイ」「ホッカイロ」などがその例です。

自然への関心も多くのオノマトペを生んできた

もともと、オノマトペとはフランス語（Onomatopée）で擬声語と擬音語のことです。擬声語は「クスクス」や「ワンワン」のように、人間や動物の声を表すものです。擬音語は「ザーザー」や「ガタガタ」のように、自然界の音や物の音を表します。これらには二音節のくり返しのパターンがよく見られます。日本語のオノマトペは、これらのほかに、物事の様子や状態を表す擬態語が非常に多いのです。擬態語は音ではなく、視覚、触覚、味覚、嗅覚に訴えます。日本人がオノマトペを好むのは、昔から四季の変化や自然の様子に大きな関心を寄せてきたからと言われています。また、英語と比べると、日本語は動詞が少なく、副詞としてニュアンスを分けるためにオノマトペが必要だったとも言われています。日本最古の歴史書『古事記』にも既にオノマトペが使われています。

日本人の感覚や日本語の特性を知るヒントになる

日本語のオノマトペを学習すると、日本人の感覚や心を知ることができます。言葉を尽くして論理的に説明するより、感覚的、情緒的な表現で相手に伝えることを好む傾向がはっきりとわかるでしょう。また、特に擬態語を知れば知るほど、英語のように「主体者が～をする」と動的に表現するのではなく、「客観的に見ると、～のようになる」と静的に表現する日本語の特性が深く理解できるようになると思います。

Conveying Nuance, Conveying Emotion

Onomatopoeias are used extremely often in Japanese, both in daily conversations and in written language. This is because they allow you to directly express what you see, feel, or think on the inside in various situations in a way that others will understand.

"She smiled「にっこり（*nikkori*）」. Her eyes were「キラキラ（*kira kira*）」, and it made my heart「ドキドキ（*dokidoki*）」." Reading this sentence makes it immediately clear that "She" is a refined and beautiful person, and that "I" have fallen in love with "her." Onomatopoeias allow you to accurately convey nuance, explaining how a person does something in a given situation without having to go on and on. They are rhythmical expressions that convey feelings in an honest, familiar way.

Used in Various Areas and Situations

It's said that there are three to five times the number of onomatopoeias in Japanese as compared to European or Chinese languages, totaling of over 10,000. In the West, onomatopoeias are primarily used by children, and it seems that when adults use them, it gives the impression that they are juvenile and uneducated. However, they are used in a variety of different fields in Japanese, such as medicine, sports, beauty, advertising, manga, and more, and they are even attracting attention in the field of cognitive science research. Many hit products have used onomatopoeias in their names. For example, there are snacks such as「ガリガリ君（*Garigari-kun*）」and「プッチンプリン（*Pucchinprin*）」, while in household goods there are「ゴキブリホイホイ（*Gokiburi Hoihoi*）」and「ホッカイロ（*Hokkairo*）」, among others.

Many Onomatopoeias Come from an Interest in Nature

Onomatopoeias originally come from the French "Onomatopée," which encompasses expressions relating to human or animal voices and sounds such as 「クスクス (*kusukusu*)」 and 「ワンワン (*wanwan*)」, as well as sounds from objects or the natural world such as 「ザーザー (*zāzā*)」 and 「ガタガタ (*gatagata*)」. In these, we often see a pattern where a two-syllable sound is repeated. In addition to these, there are also many Japanese onomatopoeias that are mimetic words, expressing the appearance or state of something. Mimetic words are not sounds, but rather appeal to the other senses such as sight, feel, taste, and smell. It is said that the Japanese people like onomatopoeias because they have traditionally had a strong interest in the changing of the seasons and the state of nature. Also, when compared to English, Japanese has few verbs, and so onomatopoeias are said to be needed to convey different nuances in an adverbial role. Even in the Kojiki, Japan's oldest history book, we can already see onomatopoeias being used.

Hints to Help You Understand Japanese People's Emotions and the Language's Distinguishing Features

Learning Japanese onomatopoeias will allow you to understand the feelings and emotions of Japanese people. They should help you gain a clear understanding of the tendency to communicate information using sensory and emotional expressions rather than through exhaustive, logical explanations. In particular, the more you learn about mimetic expressions, the better you should be able to understand the Japanese language's notable characteristic of expressing things not in a dynamic way, such as "The subject does (X)," but rather in a static way, such as "If looking at it objectively, it becomes (X)."

PART 1

動詞と一緒に使う
Together with Verbs

話す・しゃべる・言う
Conversing / Speaking / Saying

泣く
Crying

見る
Seeing

飲む
Drinking

笑う
Laughter

回す、回る
Turning

寝る
Sleeping

降る
Raining

話す・しゃべる・言う　Conversing / Speaking / Saying

ペラペラ

Perapera

Fluently / Blab

①外国語を不自由なく（途中で切れたりせず、流れるように）しゃべる様子。
②深く考えず、無責任に話す様子。

① To speak a foreign language without trouble (in a flowing manner, without stopping while speaking).
② To speak irresponsibly without thinking deeply.

Typical forms **ペラペラV**「話す」「しゃべる」、**ペラペラとV**、「**〜語はペラペラだ**」

Point ①は能力を評価するときに、②は行動の軽さへの注意や非難をするときによく使う。

① is used when evaluating someone's skills, while ② is often used when warning or criticizing someone's frivolous behavior.

---

1 Ⓐ すごいなあ、彼女。英語もドイツ語も**ペラペラ**だね。
Ⓑ フランス語も**ペラペラ**だよ。

Ⓐ *Sugoi nā, Kanojo. Ēgo mo doitsugo mo perapera dane.*
Ⓑ *Furansugo mo perapera dayo.*

Ⓐ She's amazing. She's fluent in both English and German.
Ⓑ She's fluent in French, too.

---

2 ★ 私のプライバシーを人に**ペラペラ**しゃべらないで。

★ *Watashi no puraibashī o hito ni perapera shaberanaide.*

★ Please don't blab about a person's private matters to other.

2

ぶつぶつ

Butsubutsu

Mumble / Grumble

①よく聞き取れない小さな声や話し方で言う様子。
②愚痴や不満などを影で言う様子。

① To speak in a low voice that is hard to hear.
② To complain or be dissatisfied while out of sight.

Typical forms ぶつぶつV「言う」、ぶつぶつとV

Point ①は独り言に対して使うことが多い。
① is often used when someone is speaking to themselves.

1

Ⓐ あの人、ずっと独り言を**ぶつぶつ**言ってるよ。
Ⓑ ちょっと変な人かも。

Ⓐ *Ano hito, zutto hitorigoto o butsubutsu itteru yo.*
Ⓑ *Chotto henna hito kamo.*

Ⓐ That person has been mumbling to himself for a while.
Ⓑ There might be something strange about him.

2

★ そんなに**ぶつぶつ**言うなら、やめたら？

★ *Sonnani butsubutsu iu nara, yametara?*

★ If it's going to make you grumble so much, why don't you stop?

泣(な)く　Crying

3　2

シクシク →p.142

Shikushiku

Weep

あまり声(こえ)を出(だ)さずに弱々(よわよわ)しく悲(かな)しそうに泣(な)くこと。
To cry weakly and sadly without making much sound.

Typical forms シクシクV「泣(な)く」

Point 弱々(よわよわ)しい泣(な)き方(かた)だが、ネガティブな印象(いんしょう)は与(あた)えない。
Though this is a weak way of crying, it does not assign a negative impression.

1
Ⓐ よう子(こ)は悲(かな)しかっただろうね。
Ⓑ うん…。あれからずっと、部屋(へや)で**シクシク**泣(な)いてたみたい。

Ⓐ *Yōko wa kanashikatta darō ne.*
Ⓑ *Un…. Arekara zutto, heya de shikushiku naiteta mitai.*

Ⓐ Youko must have been sad.
Ⓑ Yeah... I think she's been weeping in her room ever since then.

2
Ⓐ あの子、迷子(まいご)じゃない？
Ⓑ なんか、**シクシク**泣(な)いてるね。きっと、そうだよ。

Ⓐ *Ano ko, maigo janai?*
Ⓑ *Nanka, shikushiku naiteru ne. Kitto, sō dayo.*

Ⓐ Isn't that girl lost?
Ⓑ It looks like she's weeping. That's probably what it is.

4

わんわん
Wanwan

Howling / Barking

①大(おお)きな声(こえ)を上(あ)げて泣(な)くこと。
① To cry loudly

②犬(いぬ)の鳴(な)き声(ごえ)。
② A dog's cry

わんわんV「泣(な)く」

Point ①感情(かんじょう)のままに泣(な)くときに使(つか)う。
Used when someone lets their emotions take over as they cry.

---

1 Ⓐ 昨日(きのう)、映画(えいが)見(み)ながら**わんわん**泣(な)いちゃった。
Ⓑ そんなにいい映画(えいが)なんだ。じゃ、私(わたし)も見(み)ようかな。

Ⓐ *Kinō, ēga minagara wanwan naichatta.*
Ⓑ *Sonnani ī ēga nanda. Ja, watashi mo miyō kana.*

Ⓐ I was howling as I cried watching a movie yesterday.
Ⓑ It's that good of a movie? Maybe I should go see it too, then.

---

2 Ⓐ 負(ま)けた時(とき)は本当(ほんとう)に悔(くや)しくて、みんなで**わんわん**泣(な)きました。
Ⓑ まだ高校生(こうこうせい)だからね。

Ⓐ *Maketa toki wa hontōni kuyashikute, minna de wanwan nakimashita.*
Ⓑ *Mada kōkōsē dakara ne.*

Ⓐ We felt so truly frustrated when we lost that we started to howl and cry.
Ⓑ Well, you are still high school students. (Of course you'll cry.)

見る(み) Seeing

5 ちらっと／ちらりと

3

Chiratto / Chirarito

見(み)ていることを周(まわ)りや相手(あいて)に知(し)られないように、瞬間的(しゅんかんてき)に目(め)を向(む)けること。

To look at something so that one's surroundings or others do not notice, to look at something for a moment.

チラッとV「見(み)る」「見(み)せる」

Point 瞬間的(しゅんかんてき)に見(み)たり見(み)えたりしたときに使(つか)う。

Used when looking or seeing something for a moment.

1

Ⓐ 田中君(たなかくん)の点数(てんすう)、**ちらっと**見(み)ちゃったんだけど、100点(てん)だったよ。

Ⓑ 彼(かれ)、できるからね。

Ⓐ *Tanaka kun no tensū, chiratto michatta n da kedo, 100ten datta yo.*

Ⓑ *Kare, dekiru kara ne.*

Ⓐ I glanced at Tanaka-kun's score, and he got a 100.

Ⓑ Well, he is good.

2

Ⓐ この子(こ)、知(し)らない？ 最近(さいきん)、すごくテレビに出(で)てるよ。

Ⓑ ああ、**ちらっと**見(み)たことがある。何(なに)かのコマーシャルで。

Ⓐ *Kono ko, shiranai? Saikin, sugoku terebi ni deteru yo.*

Ⓑ *Ā, chiratto mita koto ga aru. Nanika no komāsharu de.*

Ⓐ Do you know this girl? She's been on TV all the time lately.

Ⓑ Oh, I've glanced at her before. On some sort of commercial.

6

ちらちら

Chirachira

Repeatedly glance

断続的に見ること、物が見え隠れすること。

To see intermittently, for something to be visible then hidden.

Typical forms ちらちらV「見る」「見える」

Point 相手に気づかれないように見るときに使う。

Used when looking at someone in a way where they do not notice.

1

Ⓐ さっきから何を**ちらちら**見てるの？
Ⓑ ほら、あの人。有名なタレントじゃないかな。

Ⓐ *Sakki kara nani o chirachira miteru no?*
Ⓑ *Hora, ano hito, yūmēna tarento ja nai kana.*

Ⓐ What do you keep glancing at?
Ⓑ That person over there. Isn't that a famous celebrity?

2

★ Ｔシャツのえりから下着が**ちらちら**見えてるよ。着替えたら？

★ *Tī-shatsu no eri kara shitagi ga chirachira mieteru yo. Kigaetara?*

★ I can keep on getting glimpses of your underwear from the neck of your shirt. Why don't you get changed?

7

4

じっと
Jitto

Staring

視線を動かさずに、しばらくの間、集中して見る様子。
To focus on something with one's vision without moving off of it.

Typical forms じっとV「見る」「見つめる」「する」

Point 一点に集中して見るときに使う。強調するときは「じーっと」と言う。
Used when focusing on a single point with your vision.「じーっと」is also used for emphasis.

---

1 Ⓐ あの犬、かわいい。さっきから飼い主さんのほうを**じっと**見てる。
Ⓑ 飼い主さんのことが大好きなんだね。

Ⓐ *Ano inu, kawaī. Sakki kara kainushi san no hō o jitto miteru.*
Ⓑ *Kainushi san no koto ga daisukina n dane.*

Ⓐ That dog is cute. It's been staring at its owner for a while.
Ⓑ It must love its owner.

---

2 Ⓐ さっきからあなたのことを**じっと**見ている人がいるよ。
Ⓑ え？ いやだなあ。どんな人？

Ⓐ *Sakki kara anata no koto o jitto miteiru hito ga iru yo.*
Ⓑ *E? Iyadanā. Donna hito?*

Ⓐ There's someone who has been staring at you for a while now.
Ⓑ What? I don't like that. What kind of person?

Small Steps

✲「じっと」には「動かないこと」という意味もある。
「じっと」also means "not moving."

例 あ、動かないで！ そのままそこに**じっと**していて。
A, ugokanaide! sono mama soko ni jitto shite ite.
Oh, don't move! Just stay there.

8

じろじろ

Scrutinize

Jirojiro

相手への遠慮などなく、上から下まで見ること。

To look someone from head to toe without consideration of how they may feel.

じろじろV「見る」

Point 好奇心そのままで見る様子。

To look at someone according only to one's curiosity.

---

1 Ⓐ そんなに**じろじろ**見ないで。恥ずかしいから。

Ⓑ あ、ごめん。

Ⓐ *Sonnani jirojiro minaide. Hazukashī kara.*

Ⓑ *A,gomen.*

Ⓐ Don't scrutinize me like that. It's embarrassing.

Ⓑ Oh, sorry.

---

2 ★ ここは田舎だから、外国の人は**じろじろ**見られてかわいそうだ。

★ *Koko wa inaka da kara, gaikoku no hito wa jirojiro mirarete kawaisō da.*

★ I feel bad for people from overseas, they're scrutinized here because this is the countryside.

飲む　Drinking

9 　5

ごくごく
Gokugoku

Gulp down

勢いよく、一気に飲むこと。
To vigorously drink all at once.

Typical forms　ごくごくV「飲む」、ごくごくとV

Point 勢いよく飲むときの、のどの音を表す語。
A term used to express the sound a throat makes when vigorously drinking something.

---

1 Ⓐ おいしそうにビールをごくごく飲んでる人を見ると、飲みたくなるなあ。
Ⓑ じゃ、注文する？

Ⓐ *Oishisōni bīru o gokugoku nonderu hito o miru to, nomitakunaru nā.*
Ⓑ *Ja, chūmon suru?*

Ⓐ When I see you gulping down that beer like it's delicious, it makes me want to drink one, too.
Ⓑ Will you order one, then?

---

2 ★ この牛乳、おいしくて、ごくごく飲んじゃった。

★ *Kono gyūnyū, oishikute, gokugoku nonjatta.*

★ This milk is delicious, I just gulped it down.

10

がぶがぶ

Gabugabu

Swig

人の目や結果など気にしないで、勢いよく、飲みたいだけ飲む様子。

To drink with vigor according to one's desires, not worrying about one's appearance to others or the consequences.

がぶがぶV「飲む」、**がぶがぶとV**、名詞表現で「**がぶ飲み**」

Point （暑い時に飲む）水やお酒などを飲む例が多い。

Often used when drinking water or alcohol (when it is hot).

---

1 Ⓐ なんか、お腹が痛くなってきた。

Ⓑ 冷たいものを**がぶがぶ**飲んだからじゃない？

Ⓐ *Nanka, onaka ga itaku nattekita.*

Ⓑ *Tsumetai mono o gabugabu nonda kara janai?*

Ⓐ My stomach is starting to hurt for some reason.

Ⓑ Isn't it because you took all those swigs of something cold?

---

2 ★ のど渇いてたから、水を**がぶがぶ**飲んじゃった。

★ *Nodo kawaiteta kara, mizu o gabugabu nonjatta.*

★ I took swigs of water because my throat was dry.

笑う　Laughter

11　6

ゲラゲラ
Geragera

Guffaw

人目(ひとめ)を気(き)にしないで、大声(おおごえ)で笑(わら)うこと。
To laugh loudly without being concerned about one's appearance to others.

ゲラゲラV「笑(わら)う」、**ゲラゲラとV**

Point おかしいものを見(み)たり聞(き)いたりして笑(わら)うときに使(つか)う。あまり上品(じょうひん)でない笑(わら)い方(かた)。
Used when laughing after seeing or hearing something funny. A kind of laugh that is not very refined.

1
Ⓐ ひどい！　そんなに**ゲラゲラ**笑(わら)うなんて。
Ⓑ だって、おかしいんだもの。

Ⓐ *Hidoi! Sonna ni geragera warau nante.*
Ⓑ *Datte, okashii n da mono.*

Ⓐ You're terrible! How can you guffaw like that?
Ⓑ But it's funny!

2
Ⓐ テレビ見(み)て**ゲラゲラ**笑(わら)うひまがあったら、少(すこ)し手伝(てつだ)ってよ。
Ⓑ ごめん、ごめん。

Ⓐ *Terebi mite geragera warau hima ga attara, sukoshi tetsudatte yo.*
Ⓑ *Gomen, gomen.*

Ⓐ If you have enough time to be guffawing at the TV, come help me instead.
Ⓑ Sorry, sorry.

12

クスクス

Kusukusu

Giggle

大きな声を出さずに、口も大きく開けずに、楽しそうに笑うこと。
To laugh with amusement without making a loud noise or opening one's mouth big.

クスクスV「笑う」、**クスクスとV**、**クスッ**→「〜と笑う」「〜とくる」

Point 軽く笑うときや、抑えて笑うときに使う。
Used when laughing in a slight or restrained way.

---

1 Ⓐ みんなで何**クスクス**笑ってるの？
Ⓑ 田中さんに冗談言ったのに、全然気がつかないから。

Ⓐ *Minna de nani kusukusu waratteru no?*
Ⓑ *Tanaka san ni jōdan itta noni, zenzen ki ga tsukanai kara.*

Ⓐ What's everyone giggling about?
Ⓑ We made a joke to Tanaka-san but he doesn't notice it at all.

---

2 ★ 日本の女性は、**クスクス**笑うときに口を隠す人が多いね。

★ *Nihon no josē wa, kusukusu warau toki ni kuchi o kakusu hito ga ōi ne.*

★ Many Japanese women cover their mouths when they giggle, don't they?

✻「クスッ」は、瞬間的な抑えた笑い。
「クスッ」means to laugh for a moment in a restrained way.

例 私が冗談を言ったら、石井先生も**クスッと**笑ってくれた。
Watashi ga jōdan o ittara, Ishii sensēmo kusutto waratte kureta.
Even Ishii-sensei laughed when I made a joke.

13

7

にこにこ

Nikoniko

Beam

楽(たの)しそうに、明(あか)るくほほえむ様子(ようす)。

To smile in an amused and bright way.

にこにこする、にこにこV「笑(わら)う」、にこにことV

Point 継続的(けいぞくてき)に微笑(ほほえ)んでいるときに使(つか)う。

Used when continually smiling.

---

1 Ⓐ 彼女(かのじょ)、感(かん)じがいいね。いつも**にこにこ**してて。

Ⓑ そうだね。

Ⓐ *Kanojo, kanji ga ii ne. Itsumo nikoniko shitete.*

Ⓑ *Sō da ne.*

Ⓐ I like her. She's always beaming.

Ⓑ You're right.

---

2 Ⓐ **にこにこ**笑(わら)っていると、心(こころ)も元気(げんき)になる。

Ⓑ なるべく**にこにこ**笑(わら)うようにしています。そのほうが元気(げんき)になるから。

Ⓐ *Nikoniko waratte iru to, kokoro mo genki ni naru.*

Ⓑ *Narubeku nikoniko warau yō ni shite imasu. Sono hō ga genki ni naru kara.*

Ⓐ If you have a beaming smile on your face, your heart and mind will be energized as well.

Ⓑ I'm trying to always have a beaming smile on my face. Doing that will make me more energized.

14

にっこり

Nikkori

Grin

表情をゆるめて笑顔をつくる様子。

To smile in with a relaxed expression on one's face.

にっこりする、にっこりV「笑う」「ほほえむ」、**にっこりとV**

Point 瞬間的にほほえむことについて言う。

Used when smiling for only a moment.

---

1 ★〈写真〉じゃ、2枚撮りますね。はい、みんな、**にっこり**して〜。はい、チーズ！

★ *[shashin] Ja, ni mai torimasu ne. Hai, minna, nikkori shitē. Hai, chīzu!*

★〈Photograph〉Okay, I'll take two. Alright, everyone, I want you to grin! Okay, cheese!

---

2 Ⓐ となりの部屋の人は、どんな人ですか。

Ⓑ 感じのいい人ですよ。会うと、いつも**にっこり**笑って挨拶してくれます。

Ⓐ *Tonari no heya no hito wa, donna hito desu ka?*

Ⓑ *Kanji no ī hito desu yo. Au to, itsumo nikkori waratte aisatsu shite kuremasu.*

Ⓐ What kind of person is in the next room over?

Ⓑ A likable person. He's always grinning when he greets me every time we meet.

✲ にこりともしない：決まり文句で、相手に対して全く笑顔を見せないことを表す。

A set phrase that means to not smile whatsoever at someone.

例 彼女は何を話しても、**にこりともしない**。

Kanojo wa nani o hanashitemo, nikori tomo shinai.

No matter what she's saying, she doesn't even grin.

15

ニヤニヤ

Niyaniya

Smirk

何(なに)かを考(かんが)えながら、一人(ひとり)で黙(だま)って笑(わら)う様子(ようす)。

To laugh to oneself quietly while thinking of something.

ニヤニヤする、ニヤニヤV「笑(わら)う」、ニヤニヤとV

Point これから起(お)こることを想像(そうぞう)したり、おかしいことを思(おも)い出(だ)したりしたときに笑(わら)ってしまう場合(ばあい)など。

Used when smiling while imagining what is going to happen next, remembering something funny, and so on.

1

Ⓐ 石川(いしかわ)さん、朝(あさ)からずっと**ニヤニヤ**してるよ。

Ⓑ 何(なに)かいいことでも、あったんじゃない？

Ⓐ *Ishikawa san, asa kara zutto niyaniya shiteru yo.*

Ⓑ *Nanika ī koto demo, atta n ja nai?*

Ⓐ Ishikawa-san has been smirking since this morning.

Ⓑ Maybe something good happened to her?

2

Ⓐ さっきから何(なに)、**ニヤニヤ**してるの？

Ⓑ 別(べつ)に。何(なん)でもないよ。ちょっと思(おも)い出(だ)しただけ。

Ⓐ *Sakki kara nani, niyaniya shiteru no?*

Ⓑ *Betsu ni. Nan demo nai yo. Chotto omoidashita dake.*

Ⓐ What have you been smirking about?

Ⓑ Oh, it's nothing really. I just remembered something.

回す、回る　Turning

16

くるくる
Kurukuru

Turning

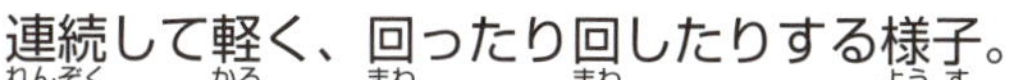

連続して軽く、回ったり回したりする様子。

To continuously turn, or to turn around and around.

くるくるV「回る」「回す」「巻く」、**くるくるとV**

Point 一回だけ回る場合には使わず、何度も回る場合に使う。
Not used when turning around just once. Used when turning around many times.

---

1 Ⓐ この窓はどうやって開けるの？
Ⓑ ああ、それはハンドルを**くるくる**回して開けるタイプだよ。

Ⓐ *Kono mado wa dōyatte akeru no?*
Ⓑ *Ā, sore wa handoru o kurukuru mawashite akeru taipu dayo.*

Ⓐ How do you open this window?
Ⓑ Oh, it's one where you open it by turning the handle.

---

2 Ⓐ あの犬、ボール遊びが好きなんだね。
Ⓑ うん。**くるくる**回って、すごくうれしそう。

Ⓐ *Ano inu, bōru asobi ga suki nan da ne.*
Ⓑ *Un. Kurukuru mawatte, sugokūreshisō.*

Ⓐ That dog likes playing with balls, doesn't it?
Ⓑ Yes. It turns around and around and seems so happy.

✲ 連続して何かを巻くときにも使う。
Also used when repeatedly wrapping around something.

例 トルティーヤにいろいろなものを入れて**くるくる**巻いてみましょう。

Torutīya nīroiro na monō irete kurukuru maite mimashō.
Try putting a lot of different things in a tortilla and wrapping it up.

17

コロコロ

Korokoro

Rolling

丸いものや小さいものが転がる様子。
Used when something round or small is rolling.

Typical forms **コロコロV**「転がる」「転がす」「太る」、**コロコロとV**

Point 小さい子供の特徴として使い、かわいらしさを表現することも多い。
Used to describe small children, and often to express cuteness.

---

1 Ⓐ あ、私の消しゴム、あんな所まで行ってる！
Ⓑ **コロコロ**転がっちゃったんだね。

Ⓐ *A, watashi no keshigomu, anna tokoro made itteru!*
Ⓑ *Korokoro korogacchatta nda ne.*

Ⓐ Oh, look at how far my eraser went!
Ⓑ It must have rolled along the floor.

---

2 Ⓐ **コロコロ**太った子犬ってかわいいね。
Ⓑ あの子犬、**コロコロ**しててかわいい。

Ⓐ *Korokoro futotta koinu tte kawaī ne.*
Ⓑ *Ano koinu, korokoro shitete kawaī.*

Ⓐ Fat puppies are so cute.
Ⓑ That puppy is round and cute.

Small Steps

✲「コロコロ」は、物事が簡単に変わることも表す。
「コロコロ」can also describe a something that changes easily.

例 部長は言うことが**コロコロ**変わるから困る。
Buchō wa iu koto ga korokoro kawaru kara komaru.
The division chief always changes what he's saying, so I don't know what to do.

18

ぐるっと

Gurutto

Twirl

一回転(いっかいてん)、または一周(いっしゅう)する様子(ようす)を表(あらわ)す。

A single turn or a single lap around.

Typical forms ぐるっとV「回(まわ)る」「回(まわ)す」「巻(ま)く」

Point 円(えん)をかくような動(うご)きについて言(い)う。

Used to describe circular movement.

---

1 Ⓐ 京都(きょうと)は行(い)きたい所(ところ)が多(おお)くて困(こま)るね。
Ⓑ バスの一日券(いちにちけん)を買(か)って、**ぐるっと**回(まわ)るのはどう？

Ⓐ *Kyōto wa ikitai tokoro gaōkute komaru ne.*
Ⓑ *Basu no ichinichi ken o katte, gurutto mawaru no wa dō?*

Ⓐ There are so many places I want to go in Kyoto that it's difficult.
Ⓑ Why don't you buy a one-day buss pass and take a lap around?

---

2 ★ 時間(じかん)があったから、この辺(へん)を**ぐるっと**してきたよ。

★ *Jikan gātta kara, konohen o gurutto shite kita yo.*

★ I had some time, so I did a lap around here.

寝る　Sleeping

19　9

ぐっすり

Gussuri

Sound Asleep

深く、よく眠る様子。

To sleep deeply and well.

ぐっすりV「寝る」、ぐっすりとV

Point 意味は good sleep と同じ。

The same as "good sleep."

---

1 Ⓐ おはよう。今日はいい顔してるね。
Ⓑ うん、昨日の夜は久しぶりに**ぐっすり**寝られたからね。

Ⓐ *Ohayō. Kyō wa ī kao shiteru ne.*
Ⓑ *Un, kinō no yoru wa hisashiburi ni gussuri nerareta kara ne.*

Ⓐ Good morning. You've got a good look on your face today.
Ⓑ Yeah, I was able to sleep soundly last night for the first time in a while.

---

2 ★ このふとん、気持ちいい！ **ぐっすり**寝られそう。

★ *Kono futon, kimochiī! Gussuri neraresō.*

★ This futon feels great! I bet I'll be able to sleep soundly on it.

20

スヤスヤ
Suyasuya

Slumber

小さな寝息を立てながら、静かに気持ちよさそうに眠る様子。
To sleep while breathing softly in a quiet and comfortable way.

スヤスヤV「寝る」、スヤスヤとV

Point 誰かが寝ている姿を見て、それを表現するときに使う。
Used to describe the way one sees someone sleep.

1
Ⓐ あの赤ちゃん、ミルク飲んだら静かになったね。
Ⓑ うん。あんなに泣いてたのに、**スヤスヤ**寝てるよ。

Ⓐ *Ano akachan, miruku nondara shizuka ni natta ne.*
Ⓑ *Un. Anna ni naiteta noni, suyasuya neteru yo.*

Ⓐ That baby got quiet once it drank its milk.
Ⓑ Yes. It was crying so much, but now it's slumbering.

2
Ⓐ 愛子はもう寝た？
Ⓑ うん。今回の旅行は長かったから、疲れたんじゃない？ **スヤスヤ**寝てる。

Ⓐ *Aiko wa mō neta?*
Ⓑ *Un. Konkai no ryokō wa nagakatta kara tsukareta n ja nai? Suyasuya neteru.*

Ⓐ Did Aiko go to sleep already?
Ⓑ Yes. She's probably tired because of how long this trip was. She's slumbering.

降る(ふ) Raining

21 ザーザー

10

Zāzā

Pouring

音(おと)を立(た)てて激(はげ)しく降(ふ)る雨(あめ)の様子(ようす)を表(あらわ)す。

Expresses rain that is coming down loudly and hard.

ザーザーV「降(ふ)る」、ザーザーとV、名詞(めいし)「ザーザー降(ぶ)り」

Point 雨(あめ)の激(はげ)しさを表(あらわ)すカジュアルな言(い)い方(かた)。

A casual way to express the intensity of rain.

---

1 Ⓐ 雨(あめ)が**ザーザー**降(ふ)ってきたよ。
Ⓑ ほんとだ。結構(けっこう)、強(つよ)いね。

Ⓐ *Ame ga zāzā futte kita yo.*
Ⓑ *Honto da. Kekkō, tsuyoi ne.*

Ⓐ The rain has started to pour.
Ⓑ You're right. It's pretty strong.

---

2 Ⓐ (窓(まど)の外(そと)を見(み)て) まだ**ザーザー**降(ふ)ってる。
Ⓑ あ、そう…。じゃ、出(で)るのは、もうちょっと後(あと)にしようか。

Ⓐ *(Mado no soto o mite) Mada zāzā futteru.*
Ⓑ *A, sō…. Ja, deru no wa, mō chotto ato ni shiyō ka.*

Ⓐ (Looking out a window) It's still pouring.
Ⓑ Oh, is it…? In that case, why don't we leave a little later.

Small Steps

✲ ザーザー降(ぶ)り：「激(はげ)しい雨(あめ)」のカジュアルな言(い)い方(かた)。

A casual way of saying "intense rain."

例 こんな**ザーザー降(ぶ)り**だと、イベント、中止(ちゅうし)になるね。

Konna zāzā buri dato, ibento, chūshi ni naru ne.

Oh, is it…? In that case, why don't we leave a little later.

22

しとしと

Shitoshito

Drizzling

雨音(あまおと)が聞(き)こえず、静(しず)かに降(ふ)り続(つづ)く雨(あめ)の様子(ようす)。

To rain constantly without making any noise.

Typical forms しとしとV「降(ふ)る」、しとしととV

Point 長(なが)く降(ふ)り続(つづ)く雨(あめ)を表(あらわ)すときによく使(つか)う。

Often used to express rain that continues on for a long time.

1

Ⓐ まだ、しとしと降(ふ)ってる。今日(きょう)は雨(あめ)、やまないね。

Ⓑ そうだね。

Ⓐ *Mada, shitoshito futteru. Kyō wā ame, yamanai ne.*

Ⓑ *Sō da ne.*

Ⓐ It's still drizzling. I don't think it'll stop today.

Ⓑ You're right.

2

Ⓐ 〈電話(でんわ)で〉そっちの天気(てんき)はどう？

Ⓑ ちょっと寒(さむ)いですね。雨(あめ)もしとしと降(ふ)ってて。

Ⓐ *〈Denwa de〉 Socchi no tenki wa dō?*

Ⓑ *Chotto samui desu ne. Ame mo shitoshito futtete.*

Ⓐ (On the phone) What's the weather like over there?

Ⓑ It's a little cold. It's drizzling rain, too.

23

11

ポツポツ

Potsupotsu

Sprinkling

雨が降り始めたことを肌に落ちる雨粒で感じた時の表現。

An expression used when one feels rain beginning to fall on their skin.

ポツポツV「降る」「くる」「落ちる」、**ポツポツとV**、名詞は「**ポツポツ雨**」

Point これから雨が強くなると感じている場合が多い。

Often used when it feels like the rain will get stronger.

1

Ⓐ あっ、**ポツポツ**降ってきた！
Ⓑ ほんとだ。どこかお店に入る？

Ⓐ *Att, Potsupotsu futte kita!*
Ⓑ *Hontoda. Dokoka omise ni hairu?*

Ⓐ Oh, it's starting to sprinkle!
Ⓑ You're right. Want to go into a store somewhere?

2

Ⓐ 雨、降り始めた？
Ⓑ うん。でも、まだ**ポツポツ**って感じ。かさは誰も差してない。

Ⓐ *Ame, furi hajimeta?*
Ⓑ *Un. Demo, mada potsupotsu tte kanji. Kasa wa dare mo sashite nai.*

Ⓐ Has it started to rain?
Ⓑ Yes. But it's still just sprinkling. No one has an umbrella out.

24

パラパラ

Pattering

Parapara

くもり空から雨が降り始め、まだ小雨の状態を表す表現。

An expression used to describe rain beginning to come down from the clouds or a small shower.

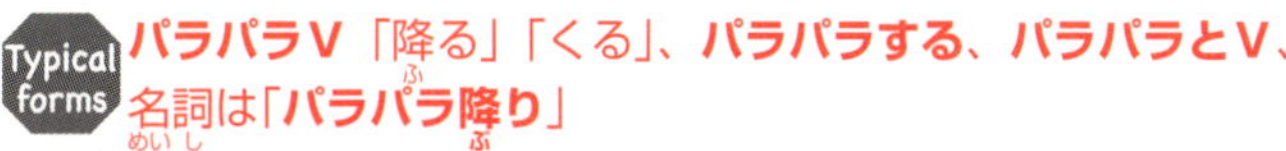
Typical forms **パラパラV**「降る」「くる」、**パラパラする**、**パラパラとV**、名詞は「**パラパラ降り**」

Point「ポツポツ」より少し多く、軽く音がする雨に使う。

Used for rain that is greater in amount than「ポツポツ」but also quiet.

---

1 Ⓐ〈電話で〉もしもし、そっちの天気、どう？

Ⓑ うん、**パラパラ**降ってるよ。

Ⓐ *〈Denwa de〉Moshimoshi, socchi no tenki, dō?*

Ⓑ *Un, parapara futteru yo.*

Ⓐ (On the phone)
Hello, how is the weather over there?

Ⓑ Oh, it's pattering rain right now.

---

2 ★〈キャンプで〉**パラパラ**来たら、急いでテントを張ったほうがいいね。

★ *〈Kyanpu de〉Parapara kitara, isoide tento o hatta hō ga ī ne.*

★ (At a camp)
If it starts pattering, we should probably pitch a tent quickly.

PART 2

動作や変化の特徴を表す

Expressing the Characteristics of an Action or Change

やり方
Method

正しく、確実に
Correctly, Soundly

勢い
Vigorously

スムーズ
Smoothly

一斉に、一気に
All at Once

少しずつ
Gradually

遅い
Slow

音
Sound

不安定
Uncertainty

隠れて
Hiding

その他
Other

やり方(かた) Method

さっと
Satto

Quickly

急(いそ)いで、早(はや)く何(なに)かをすること。

To do something quickly and in a hurry.

さっとV「やる」「帰(かえ)る」「拭(ふ)く」

Point 動作(どうさ)が早(はや)く行(おこな)われることを強調(きょうちょう)する表現(ひょうげん)。

An expression used to emphasize an action conducted quickly.

1
Ⓐ あの人(ひと)、5時(じ)になると、**さっと**帰(かえ)るね。
Ⓑ 気(き)がつくと、もう、いないよね。

Ⓐ *Ano hito, go-ji ni naruto, satto kaeru ne.*
Ⓑ *Ki ga tsukuto, mō, inai yo ne.*

Ⓐ That person leaves quickly once it's five, doesn't he?
Ⓑ Yes, he's gone by the time I notice.

2
Ⓐ テーブルもきれいにしないとね。
Ⓑ うん。でも、**さっと**拭(ふ)くだけでいいよ。

Ⓐ *Tēburu mo kirē ni shinaito ne.*
Ⓑ *Un. Demo, satto fuku dake de ī yo.*

Ⓐ I need to clean the table, don't I?
Ⓑ Yes. But you just need to wipe it down quickly

2

ざっと

Zatto

Roughly

細かいところは気にせず、大まかである様子。

To do something in a broad way, unconcerned about the details.

Typical forms ざっとV「見る」「やる」、助数詞を伴う名詞「ざっと〜個」

Point 大まかだが、一通りやるときに使う。

Used when doing something in a general but broad way.

---

1 Ⓐ この書類に**ざっと**目を通しといて。
Ⓑ はい、わかりました。

Ⓐ *Kono shorui ni zatto me o tōshi toite.*
Ⓑ *Hai, wakarimashita.*

Ⓐ Just skim over this document.
Ⓑ Okay, I will.

---

2 ★ 駐車場には車が**ざっと**30台ありました。

★ *Chūshajō ni wa kuruma ga zatto sanjū-dai arimashita.*

★ There were roughly 30 cards in the parking lot.

13

すっと →p.197

Sutto

Quietly

早(はや)く、滞(とどこお)らずに動作(どうさ)や変化(へんか)が起(お)きる様子(ようす)。

An action or change that takes place in a fast and prompt way.

Typical forms **すっとV** 「消(き)える」「現(あらわ)れる」「出(だ)す」

Point 目立(めだ)たず、さりげない感(かん)じ。

This term gives an inconspicuous connotation to an action.

---

1 Ⓐ〈マッサージの後(あと)〉どうですか。

Ⓑ はい、体(からだ)が**すっと**軽(かる)くなりました。

Ⓐ *[Massāji no ato] Dō desu ka?*

Ⓑ *Hai, karada ga sutto karuku nari mashita.*

Ⓐ (After a massage) How was it?

Ⓑ Well, my body suddenly feels much lighter.

---

2 Ⓐ 田中(たなか)さんは帰(かえ)ったんだ。

Ⓑ ええ。ずっと一緒(いっしょ)にいたけど、いつの間(ま)にか、**すっと**消(き)えていたんです。

Ⓐ *Tanaka san wa kaetta n da.*

Ⓑ *Ē. Zutto issho nīta kedo, itsu no ma ni ka, sutto kiete ita n desu.*

Ⓐ So Tanaka-san went home?

Ⓑ Yes. I was with him the whole time, but he quietly disappeared before I noticed.

4

そっと
Sotto

Softly

人(ひと)に気(き)づかれないように、静(しず)かに何(なに)かをすること。
To do something in a quiet way so as not to be noticed by others.

Typical forms そっとV「置(お)く」「閉(し)める」「出(で)る」

Point 音(おと)を立(た)てないように、干渉(かんしょう)しないようにする様子(ようす)。
To do something in a way that makes no noise so as not to interfere with others.

---

1 ★ みんな、もう寝(ね)ていたので、ドアを**そっと**開(あ)けた。

★ *Minna, mō nete ita node, doa o sotto aketa.*

★ Everyone was asleep already, so I softly opened the door.

---

2 Ⓐ 彼女(かのじょ)、失恋(しつれん)したんでしょう？　みんなでなぐさめようか。
Ⓑ いや、**そっと**してあげたほうがいいよ。

Ⓐ *Kanojo, shitsuren shita n deshō? Minna de nagusame yō ka.*
Ⓑ *Iya, sotto shite ageta hō ga ī yo.*

Ⓐ She had her heart broken, right? We should all comfort her.
Ⓑ No, I think we shouldn't make a big deal of it.

5

14

てきぱき

Tekipaki

Briskly

物事(ものごと)を無駄(むだ)なく早(はや)く、上手(じょうず)にする様子(ようす)。

To do something in an efficient, quick, and skilled way.

てきぱきV「働(はたら)く」「動(うご)く」、てきぱきとV

Point 仕事(しごと)のやり方(かた)について言(い)うときによく使(つか)う。

Often used when talking about how a job is performed.

---

1 Ⓐ ずいぶん時間(じかん)かかってるけど、もう少(すこ)し**てきぱき**できない？

Ⓑ すみません…。

Ⓐ *Zuibun jikan kakatteru kedo, mō sukoshi tekipaki deki nai?*

Ⓑ *Sumimasen….*

Ⓐ It's taking quite a bit of time, can't you do it a little more briskly?

Ⓑ I'm sorry...

---

2 ★ 面接(めんせつ)のときは、質問(しつもん)に**てきぱき**と答(こた)えたほうがいいよ。

★ *Mensetsu no toki wa. shitsumon ni tekipaki to kotaeta hō ga ī yo.*

★ When you're being interviewed, you should reply to questions briskly.

6

わざわざ

Wazawaza

Expressly

ふつうはする必要がないのに、特に時間と手間をかけてする様子。

To take the time and effort to do something that is normally not done.

Typical forms わざわざV

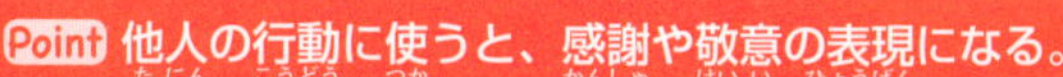

Point 他人の行動に使うと、感謝や敬意の表現になる。

Becomes an expression of thanks or respect when used about someone else's actions.

1 Ⓐ 忙しいのに、**わざわざ**来てくれてありがとう。

Ⓑ いえ、どういたしまして。

Ⓐ *Isogashī noni, wazawaza kite kurete arigatō.*

Ⓑ *Ie, dō itashi mashite.*

Ⓐ Thank you for taking the time to come when you're busy.

Ⓑ No, thank you.

2 Ⓐ **わざわざ**重い物を運んであげたのに、礼も言わないなんて。

Ⓑ そういう人なんだよ。

Ⓐ *Wazawaza omoi mono o hakonde ageta noni, rēmo iwanai nante.*

Ⓑ *Sō iu hito nanda yo.*

Ⓐ You went out of your way to carry that heavy thing, but they didn't even thank you.

Ⓑ That's the kind of person they are.

正しく、確実に　Correctly, Soundly

7　15

きちんと

Properly

Kichinto

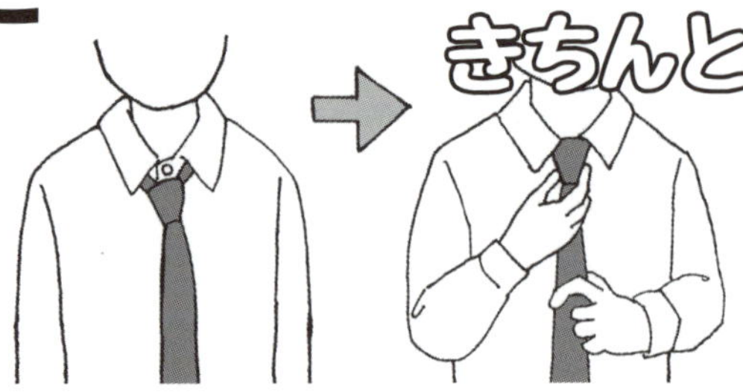

決められたとおり、正確に物事を行う様子。

To do things in an established and accurate way.

きちんとV「やる」「返す」「片づける」、**きちんとする**

Point よく整っていて、乱れがないこと。

To be well composed and not disturbed.

---

1 Ⓐ 時間通り**きちんと**来てくださいね。
Ⓑ はい、わかりました。

Ⓐ *Jikan dōri kichinto kite kudasai ne.*
Ⓑ *Hai, wakarimashita.*

Ⓐ Please come according to the time stated.
Ⓑ Alright, I understand.

---

2 ★ 入学式だから、**きちんと**した服を着ようと思います。

★ *Nyūgakushiki dakara, kichinto shita fuku o kiyō tōmoimasu.*

★ This is an entrance ceremony, so I'm thinking of wearing proper clothes.

Small Steps

✲ きちっと：「きちんと」と同じ意味で、会話でよく使われる。

Often used in conversations. A term that means the same thing as「きちんと」.

例 約束なんだから、**きちっと**守ってください。

Yakusoku nan dakara, kichitto mamotte kudasai.

It's a promise, so please uphold it properly.

8

ちゃんと

Chanto

Correctly

やるべきことを不足(ふそく)なくやる様子(ようす)。まじめで、期待(きたい)に反(はん)しないこと。

To do what needs to be done in a complete way. Serious and according to expectations.

Typical forms **ちゃんとV**「やる」「考(かんが)える」、**ちゃんとする**

Point やるべきことをやることについて言(い)うことが多(おお)い。

Often used when talking about doing something that needs to be done.

---

1 Ⓐ **ちゃんと**宿題(しゅくだい)やりなさいね。
Ⓑ はい。

Ⓐ *Chanto shukudai yarinasai ne.*
Ⓑ *Hai.*

Ⓐ Please do your homework properly.
Ⓑ Okay.

---

2 ★ 彼(かれ)は**ちゃんと**した人(ひと)だから、大丈夫(だいじょうぶ)だよ。頼(たの)んでみたら？

★ *Kare wa chanto shita hito dakara, daijōbu da yo. Tanonde mitara?*

★ He's a put-together person, so it's okay. Why not ask him?

9

16

しっかり

Firmly

Shikkari

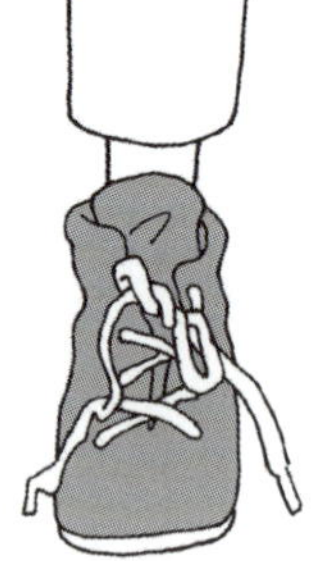

気持ち(きも)や動作(どうさ)などが強(つよ)く、確(たし)かである様子(ようす)。

Used to describe feelings or actions that are strong and certain.

Typical forms しっかりする、しっかりV「勉強(べんきょう)する」「説明(せつめい)する」

Point 「不安定(ふあんてい)」「ゆるい」などの面(めん)がなく、「固(かた)い」「安定(あんてい)」「確(たし)か」などの特徴(とくちょう)を表(あらわ)す。

Expresses firmness, stability, and certainty, or a lack of uncertainty or looseness.

---

1 Ⓐ あの子、**しっかり**しているね。
Ⓑ そうなんです。まだ若(わか)いですが、頼(たよ)りになります。

Ⓐ *Anoko, shikkari shite iru ne.*
Ⓑ *Sō nan desu. Mada wakai desu ga, tayori ni narimasu.*

Ⓐ She really has it together.
Ⓑ That's right. She's still young, but she's reliable.

---

2 Ⓐ このバンド、いいね。
Ⓑ うん。曲(きょく)もいいし、演奏(えんそう)も**しっかり**してる。

Ⓐ *Kono bando, ī ne.*
Ⓑ *Un. Kyoku mo ī shi, ensō mo shikkari shiteru.*

Ⓐ This band is nice.
Ⓑ Yes. Their songs are good, and their performances are well put together.

10

Steadily

落ち着いてゆっくり物事をする様子。

To do things in a calm and relaxed way.

Point 時間をかけ、慎重に物事をするときによく使う。

Often used to describe taking one's time to do things in a deliberate way.

1

Ⓐ 就職するか、進学するか、もう決めた？
Ⓑ まだ。**じっくり**考えて決めるよ。

Ⓐ *Shūshoku suru ka, shingaku suru ka mō kimeta?*
Ⓑ *Mada. Jikkuri kangaete kimeru yo.*

Ⓐ Have you decided whether you'll get a job or continue in your education?
Ⓑ Not yet. I'm going to take my time and decide.

2

★ あわてないで、**じっくり**話し合ったほうがいいと思います。

★ *Awatenaide, jikkuri hanashi atta hō ga ī tōmoimasu.*

★ Instead of panicking, you should take your time and talk it out.

11

きっぱり

Kippari

Clearly

態度をはっきりさせ、強い調子で明確に何かを決める様子。

To have a clear attitude and to decide on something in a strong and certain way.

きっぱりV「断る」「する」「あきらめる」、**きっぱりとV**

Point 強い意志を持って発言するときに使う。

Used when one has a strong will as they state something.

---

1 Ⓐ あの話、結局どうした？
Ⓑ ああ、**きっぱり**断りました。

Ⓐ *Ano hanashi, kekkyoku dō shita?*
Ⓑ *Ā, kippari kotowarimashita.*

Ⓐ What ever happened to that topic?
Ⓑ Oh, I clearly declined.

---

2 ★ 今でも彼女のことは好きですが、**きっぱり**とあきらめました。

★ *Ima demo kanojo no koto wa suki desu ga, kippari to akiramemashita.*

★ I still like her, but I've completely given up.

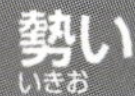

勢い Vigorously

12

どんどん
Dondon

Rapidly

妨げるものがなく、物事が勢いよく進む様子。
For things to proceed in a vigorous way, with nothing in their way.

Typical forms どんどんV「進める」「上がる」、どんどんとV

Point「どんどん〜する」は、遠慮やちゅうちょがなく、積極的な様子を表す。
「どんどん〜する」describes an assertive state, with no hesitation or indecision.

1 Ⓐ いい企画ですね。どんどん進めてください。
Ⓑ はい、ありがとうございます。

Ⓐ *Ī kikaku desu ne. Dondon susumete kudasai.*
Ⓑ *Hai, Arigatō gozaimasu.*

Ⓐ What a good plan. You should move it forward rapidly.
Ⓑ Alright, thank you.

2 ★ テレビで大きく紹介されたから、これからどんどん売れると思います。

★ *Terebi de ōkiku shōkai sareta kara, korekara dondon ureru to omoimasu.*

★ I think sales will come rapidly because we were introduced in a major way on television.

13

グングン

Gungun

{Grow} Vigorously

物事が勢いよく伸びる様子。
For something to grow vigorously.

Typical forms グングンV「伸びる」「成長する」、グングンとV

Point 加速して伸びている感じ。
Describes something that grows in an accelerating way.

1 Ⓐ 大阪支店は調子がいいですね。売上がグングン伸びてますよ。
Ⓑ へえ、うらやましいなあ。

Ⓐ *Ōsaka shiten wa chōshi ga ī desu ne. Uriage ga gungun nobite masu yo.*
Ⓑ *Hē, urayamashī nā.*

Ⓐ The Osaka branch is doing well. Sales are growing vigorously.
Ⓑ Huh, how enviable.

2 ★ 男の子は中学生になると、背がグングン伸びる。

★ *Otoko no ko wa chūgakusē ni naru to, se ga gungun nobiru.*

★ When boys reach middle school, they grow in height vigorously.

スムーズ Smoothly

14 18

すらすら

Surasura

Smoothly

困難(こんなん)がなく、なめらかに物事(ものごと)が進(すす)む様子(ようす)。

For things to proceed without trouble and smoothly.

すらすらV「読(よ)める」「書(か)ける」「話(はな)せる」、**すらすらとV**

Point「すらすら読(よ)む」「すらすら書(か)く」が典型的(てんけいてき)な例(れい)。

Reading and writing are typical use examples.

---

1 Ⓐ 漢字(かんじ)が**すらすら**読(よ)める外国人(がいこくじん)、増(ふ)えましたね。

Ⓑ そうですね。すごいですよね。

Ⓐ *Kanji ga surasura yomeru gaikokujin, fuemashita ne.*

Ⓑ *Sō desu ne. Sugoi desu yo ne.*

Ⓐ The number of foreigners who can read kanji smoothly have increased, haven't they?

Ⓑ That's right. It's amazing, isn't it?

---

2 ★ あんなふうに筆(ふで)で**すらすら**書(か)けたらいいなあ。

★ *Anna fū ni fude de surasura kaketara ī nā.*

★ It would be nice if I could write with a brush smoothly like that.

15

サクサク

Sakusaku

Easily

軽快に気持ちよく物事が進む様子。

For things to proceed in an easy and comfortable way.

サクサクV「やる」、**サクサクとV**

Point 仕事や作業について使う表現。

Used when discussing jobs or work.

---

1 Ⓐ この本を使うと、練習問題が**サクサク**できるよ。

Ⓑ へえ、そうなんだ。

Ⓐ *Kono hon o tsukau to, renshū mondai ga sakusaku dekiru yo.*

Ⓑ *Hē, sō nanda.*

Ⓐ If you use this book, you can easily go through practice questions.

Ⓑ Huh, really?

---

2 ★ 体の調子がいいので、仕事が**サクサク**片づいた。

★ *Karada no chōshi ga ī node, shigoto ga sakusaku katazuita.*

★ I feel well, so I was able to easily take care of work.

一斉(いっせい)に、一気(いっき)に　All at Once

16　19

がらりと／がらっと

Gararito/Garatto

Suddenly

それまでの状態(じょうたい)や性質(せいしつ)と大(おお)きく、急激(きゅうげき)に変(か)わる様子(ようす)。

A major, sudden change in state or nature.

がらりとV「変(か)わる」「変(か)える」

Point 良(よ)い変化(へんか)にも悪(わる)い変化(へんか)にも使(つか)う。
Used for both good and bad changes.

---

1 Ⓐ わあ、同(おな)じ店(みせ)とは思(おも)えないね。
Ⓑ ほんとだ。インテリアが**がらりと**変(か)わったね。

Ⓐ *Wā, onaji mise towa omoe nai ne.*
Ⓑ *Honto da. Interia ga gararito kawatta ne.*

Ⓐ Wow, I never would have thought that this is the same store.
Ⓑ You're right. The interior has suddenly changed.

---

2 ★ あの人(ひと)、留学(りゅうがく)してから**がらりと**人(ひと)が変(か)わったみたい。

★ *Ano hito, ryūgaku shite kara gararito hito ga kawatta mitai.*

★ It seems that her personality changed suddenly after she studied abroad.

17

ずらりと／ずらっと

Lined up

Zurarito/ Zuratto

多くの物や人が列になって一斉に並ぶ様子。

For many things or people to be lined up in a row.

ずらりV「並ぶ」「並べる」「ある」、**ずらりとV**

Point 魅力的に見えたり、感心したりするときに使う。

Used when the sight is appealing or admirable.

---

1 Ⓐ さすが一流ホテルだね。高級車が**ずらりと**並んでる。
Ⓑ ほんとだ。

Ⓐ *Sasuga ichiryū hoteru da ne. Kōkyūsha ga zurarito naranderu.*
Ⓑ *Honto da.*

Ⓐ That's a first-rate hotel for you. Luxury cars all lined up.
Ⓑ You're right.

---

2 ★ リストを見たら、有名な人の名前が**ずらっと**あった。

★ *Risutō mitara, yūmēna hito no namae ga zuratto atta.*

★ When I looked at the list, I saw a lineup of famous people's names.

18 (20)

どっと
Dotto

Burst; Wave

人や物が急にたくさん押し寄せる様子。
For people or things to suddenly descend on a location.

Typical forms どっとV「押し寄せる」「沸く」など

Point 勢いよく、一気に変化が起きたときに使う。
Used when a change suddenly and vigorously occurs.

---

1 Ⓐ お疲れさま！　大変だったね。
Ⓑ うん、**どっと**疲れたよ。

Ⓐ *Otsukare sama!　Taihendatta ne.*
Ⓑ *Un, dotto tsukareta yo.*

Ⓐ Great work! That must have been hard.
Ⓑ Yes, a wave of fatigue came down on me.

---

2 ★ 空港にファンが**どっと**押し寄せた。

★ *Kūkō ni fan ga dotto oshiyoseta.*

★ A wave of fans crowded them at the airport.

✲ みんなで一斉に声を上げる場合にも使う。
Also used when a group all raises their voices at once.

例 彼のその一言に、**どっと**笑いが起きた。
Kare no sono hitokoto ni, dotto warai ga okita.
The one thing he said caused a wave of laughter.

19

パッと

Patto

n a flash

瞬間的に新たな変化が起きる様子。

For a new change to occur in the blink of an eye.

Typical forms パッとV「広がる」「明るくなる」

Point 何かが一気に展開するときに使う。

Used when something expands all at once.

---

1 Ⓐ 見て、この花。今朝、**パッと**咲いたの。
Ⓑ ほんとだ。咲くのは来週かな、と思ってたけど。

Ⓐ *Mite, kono hana. Kesa, patto saita no.*
Ⓑ *Honto da. Saku no wa raishū kana, to omotteta kedo.*

Ⓐ Look at this flower. It bloomed in a flash this morning.
Ⓑ You're right. I had thought it might bloom next week.

---

2 Ⓐ そのうわさ、**パッと**広まったね。
Ⓑ うん。もう、みんな知ってると思う。

Ⓐ *Sono uwasa, patto hiromatta ne.*
Ⓑ *Un. Mō, minna shitteru to omou.*

Ⓐ That rumor spread in a flash.
Ⓑ Yeah. I think everyone knows about it now.

少(すこ)しずつ Gradually

20 (21)

コツコツ
Kotsukotsu

Untiringly

急(いそ)がないけど休(やす)まず、少(すこ)しずつ何(なに)かを積(つ)み上(あ)げるように努力(どりょく)し続(つづ)ける様子(ようす)。

For an effort to continue without resting as it slowly builds upon itself, though not in a rushed way.

Typical forms **コツコツV**「やる」「励(はげ)む」、**コツコツとV**

Point 継続的(けいぞくてき)な努力(どりょく)について言(い)う。
Used to describe a continuous effort.

---

1 Ⓐ 優勝(ゆうしょう)おめでとうございます。
Ⓑ ありがとうございます。**コツコツ**と練習(れんしゅう)してきてよかったです。

Ⓐ *Yūshō omedetō gozaimasu.*
Ⓑ *Arigatō gozaimasu. Kotsukotsu to renshū shite kite yokatta desu.*

Ⓐ Congratulations on the victory.
Ⓑ Thank you. I'm glad that we untiringly practiced.

---

2 ★ あの人(ひと)はどんな仕事(しごと)でも、**コツコツ**努力(どりょく)をする人(ひと)ですね。

★ *Ano hito wa donna shigoto demo, kotsukotsu doryoku o suru hito desu ne.*

★ No matter what the job, that person is the type to untiringly work at it, aren't they?

21

じわじわ

Gradually

Jiwajiwa

物事がゆっくり確実に進む様子。

For things to proceed in a slow and certain way.

じわじわV「増える」「迫る」、**じわじわとV**

Point ある傾向について言う表現。

Used to describe tendencies.

---

1 Ⓐ これは便利なサービスですね。
Ⓑ ええ。若い女性を中心に、利用者が**じわじわ**増えています。

Ⓐ *Kore wa benrina sābisu desu ne.*
Ⓑ *Ē. Wakai josē o chūshin ni, riyōsha ga jiwajiwa fuete imasu.*

Ⓐ This is such a convenient service, isn't it?
Ⓑ Yes. The number of users is gradually increasing, primarily young women.

---

2 ★ 締め切りの日が**じわじわ**迫ってきて、焦っています。

★ *Shimekiri no hi ga jiwajiwa sematte kite, asette imasu.*

★ The deadline is gradually approaching, so I'm fretting.

22

ぞろぞろ

amingly

Zorozoro

人や虫などが同じ方向に続いてゆっくり動く様子。

For people or bugs to all move slowly in the same direction.

ぞろぞろV「出る」「続く」、**ぞろぞろとV**

Point きれいにそろった動きではない。

This is not used to describe a neatly lined up movement.

---

1 Ⓐ 会場から人が**ぞろぞろ**出てくるね。
Ⓑ ああ、コンサートが終わったところなんだね。

Ⓐ *Kaijō kara hito ga zorozoro dete kuru ne.*
Ⓑ *Ā, konsāto ga owatta tokoro nanda ne.*

Ⓐ People are streaming out of that site.
Ⓑ Yes, a concert must have just ended.

---

2 ★ 出発時間が近づいたので、みんな、**ぞろぞろ**集まってきた。

★ *Shuppatsu jikan ga chikazuita node, minna, zorozoro atsumatte kita.*

★ The departure time is near, so everyone has streamed together.

遅(おそ)い　Slow

23　22

のろのろ

Lazily

Noronoro

動(うご)きが鈍(にぶ)く、ゆっくりな様子(ようす)。

Dull, slow movements.

のろのろV「する」、**のろのろとV**、名詞(めいし)「**のろのろ運転(うんてん)**」

Point 進(すす)み方(かた)が遅(おそ)くて不快(ふかい)に感(かん)じるときに使(つか)う。

Used when something or someone moves ahead in a slow and unpleasant way.

1
Ⓐ 何(なに)**のろのろ**しているの？　早(はや)くして。
Ⓑ うん、もうちょっと待(ま)って。

Ⓐ *Nani noronoro shite iru no? Hayaku shite.*
Ⓑ *Un, mō chotto matte.*

Ⓐ Why are you lazing about? Hurry up.
Ⓑ Yes, just wait a bit longer.

2
Ⓐ **のろのろ**してると、ほかの人に彼女(かのじょ)をとられちゃうよ。
Ⓑ え？　それはいやです。

Ⓐ *Noronoro shiteru to, hokano hito ni kanojō torarechau yo.*
Ⓑ *E? Sore wa iya desu.*

Ⓐ Keep lazing about and someone else will take her.
Ⓑ What? I don't want that happening.

24

グズグズ

Guzuguzu

Dawdle

判断や動作が遅く、むだに時間がかかる様子。

For a decision or action to be slow and take a needless amount of time.

グズグズする、グズグズV「言う」、グズグズとV

Point しようと思えばできるのに、すぐにしようとしない場合に使うことが多い。

Often used in cases where something could be done if wanted, but a choice is made to not do it immediately.

---

1 Ⓐ 休みの日は、朝すぐに起きれなくて、つい、ベッドで**グズグズ**しちゃう。
Ⓑ わかる、わかる。

Ⓐ *Yasumi no hi wa asa sugu ni okirenakute, tsui, beddo de guzuguzu shichau.*
Ⓑ *Wakaru, wakaru.*

Ⓐ On days off, I can't wake up immediately in the morning and find myself dawdling in bed.
Ⓑ I completely understand.

---

2 Ⓐ あの二人、早く結婚すればいいのに。
Ⓑ 彼が**グズグズ**しているから、だめなんだよ。

Ⓐ *Ano futari, hayaku kekkon sureba ī noni.*
Ⓑ *Kare ga guzuguzu shiteiru kara, dame nanda yo.*

Ⓐ Those two should just hurry up and get married.
Ⓑ It's no good because he's dawdling.

25

だらだら

Daradara

Idly

気分(きぶん)や行動(こうどう)のしかたがゆるい状態(じょうたい)。

To feel or do something in a lax way.

だらだらする、だらだらV「過(す)ごす」

Point 怠(なま)けたり、むだにゆっくりしたりするイメージ。

Conjures an image of laziness or doing something in a pointlessly slow way.

---

1 Ⓐ **だらだら**しないで、早(はや)くやってよ。
Ⓑ わかったから、ちょっと待(ま)って。

Ⓐ *Daradara shinaide, hayaku yatte yo.*
Ⓑ *Wakatta kara, chotto matte.*

Ⓐ Stop idling around and do it already.
Ⓑ I get it, just wait a second.

---

2 ★ こう暑(あつ)いと、つい、**だらだら**しちゃう。

★ *Kō atsui to, tsui, daradara shichau.*

★ I start acting idly without realizing it when it's this hot.

音(おと) Sound

26 トントン Tonton

23

Knocking

物(もの)を軽(かる)くたたいたときの音(おと)。
The sound of tapping on something lightly.

トントンV「たたく」、トントンとV、名詞(めいし)「トントン拍子(びょうし)」(順調(じゅんちょう)に進(すす)むこと)

Point 肩(かた)や背中(せなか)を軽(かる)く続(つづ)けてたたくときや、階段(かいだん)を上下(じょうげ)する足音(あしおと)にも使(つか)う。
Also used when lightly and continuously tapping on one's shoulders or back, or the sound of footsteps on stairs.

1 Ⓐ ドアを**トントン**とたたいてみて。
Ⓑ たたいてみたけど、誰(だれ)もいないみたい。

Ⓐ *Doa o tonton to tataite mite.*
Ⓑ *Tataite mita kedo, dare mo inai mitai.*

Ⓐ Try knocking on the door.
Ⓑ I tried, but it seems like no one is there.

2 ★ 肩(かた)を**とんとん**とたたかれたので、振(ふ)り返(かえ)ったら、青木(あおき)さんだった。

★ *Kata o tonton to tatakareta node, furikaettara, Aoki-san datta.*

★ Someone knocked on my shoulders, and when I looked around, it was Aoki-san.

Small Steps

✲ トントン拍子(びょうし):物事(ものごと)が調子(ちょうし)よく進(すす)むことを表(あらわ)す慣用句(かんようく)。
An idiom used to describe things proceeding well.

例 彼(かれ)は**トントン拍子(びょうし)**に出世(しゅっせ)したよね。
Kare wa tonton byōshi ni shusse shita yo ne.
He was promoted at every turn, wasn't he?

27

ドンドン

Dondon

Booming

物を続けて強くたたいたり、打ったりするときの音。

The sound made when something is continuously beaten or hit with force.

Typical forms **ドンドンV**「たたく」「打つ」、**ドンドンとV**

Point 低くて大きな音に使う。ノック音の場合は乱暴な印象を与える。
Used to describe low and loud sounds. When used to describe knocks, it gives a rough and violent impression.

1 Ⓐ 何か**ドンドン**打つ音、聞こえない？
Ⓑ ああ、あれは隣の幼稚園で太鼓をたたいているんだよ。

Ⓐ *Nani ka dondon utsu oto, kikoe nai?*
Ⓑ *Ā, are wa tonari no yōchien de taiko o tataite iru n da yo.*

Ⓐ Don't you hear a booming sound?
Ⓑ Yes, that's the sound of taiko drums being played at the kindergarten next door.

2 Ⓐ 誰？　あんなにドアを**ドンドン**叩いて。
Ⓑ ひろしちゃんよ。ほら、「こんにちは！」って言ってる。

Ⓐ *Dare? Anna ni doa o dondon tataite.*
Ⓑ *Hiroshi chan yo. Hora, "Konnichiwa!" tte itteru.*

Ⓐ Who is banging on the door like that?
Ⓑ It's Hiroshi-chan. See, he's saying "Hello!"

28

ガンガン →p.146

Gangan

大きな音や声が響いて、やかましい様子。

Loud sounds or voices ringing in a noisy way.

Typical forms **ガンガンV**「打つ」「たたく」「響く」、**ガンガンとV**

Point 頭の中で音がやかましく響く感じ。頭痛を表すときにも使う。

Used to describe sounds that ring noisily in one's head. Also used to describe a headache.

---

1 Ⓐ 工事の音が**ガンガン**響いて、頭が痛くなる。
Ⓑ うん…。早く終わってほしいね。

Ⓐ *Kōji nōto ga gangan hibīte, atama ga itaku naru.*
Ⓑ *Un…. Hayaku owatte hoshī ne.*

Ⓐ The clanging construction makes my head hurt.
Ⓑ Yes... I hope it ends soon.

---

2 ★ 先生の怒鳴り声が教室中に**ガンガン**響いた。

★ *Sensē no donarigoe ga kyōshitsu jū ni gangan hibīta.*

★ The teacher's angry voice echoed around the classroom.

Small Steps

「遠慮しないで勢いよく」などの意味もある。

Also used to mean "Vigorously, without hesitance."

例 好きな音楽を**ガンガン**かけて、みんなで踊りました。

Sukina ongaku o gangan kakete, minna de odorimashita.

We went on and played our favorite music and danced together.

29

24

バタバタ

Batabata

Flapping

①固定された物が、風に吹かれて音を立てながら動く様子。
②鳥の羽が立てる大きな音。

① For something fixed in place to make noise and move around when being blown by wind.
② Loud sounds made by a bird's wings.

バタバタする、バタバタV「音を立てる」、バタバタとV

Point 手や足を激しく動かすことや、忙しくて落ち着かないことも表す。
Also used to describe furiously moving one's arms or legs, or to be so busy that things do not calm down.

---

1 Ⓐ 鳥小屋に猫かなんか入ったんじゃない？
Ⓑ そうかも。鳥が**バタバタ**してる音が聞こえたね。

Ⓐ *Torigoya ni neko ka nan ka haitta n ja nai?*
Ⓑ *Sō kamo. Tori ga batabata shiteru oto ga kikoeta ne.*

Ⓐ Couldn't a cat have gotten into the henhouse?
Ⓑ Maybe. I can hear the birds flapping around.

---

2 ★ 風が強くて、テントが**バタバタ**音を立てている。

★ *Kaze ga tsuyokute, tento ga batabata otō o tatete iru.*

★ The wind is strong, so the tent is making sound flapping around.

✲ バタバタする：忙しく、落ち着かない様子を表す。
Used to describe a busy situation that does not calm down.

例 来週引っ越しなので**バタバタして**いる。
Raishū hikkoshi nanode, batabata shite iru.
Things have been hectic because I'm moving next week.

30

ガタガタ

Gatagata

Rattling

硬(かた)いものが風(かぜ)や力(ちから)を受(う)けて揺(ゆ)れ動(うご)くときの音(おと)。小刻(こきざ)みに震(ふる)える様子(ようす)。

The sound of something hard being moved around because of wind or an external force. For something to shake minutely.

Typical forms **ガタガタする、ガタガタV「揺(ゆ)れる」**

Point 大(おお)きな音(おと)や大(おお)きな震(ふる)えは「ガタガタ」、小(ちい)さい場合(ばあい)は「カタカタ」を使(つか)う。

「ガタガタ」is used for loud sounds or major shaking, while「カタカタ」is used in smaller cases.

1 Ⓐ 風(かぜ)が吹(ふ)くと窓(まど)が**ガタガタ**するね。
Ⓑ この建物(たてもの)、相当古(そうとうふる)そうだからね。

Ⓐ *Kaze ga fuku to mado ga gatagata suru ne.*
Ⓑ *Kono tatemono, sōtō furusō dakara ne.*

Ⓐ When the wind blows, the windows start to rattle.
Ⓑ Yes, this building is quite old.

2 ★ その時(とき)はほんとに寒(さむ)くて、**ガタガタ**震(ふる)えてました。

★ *Sono toki wa honto ni samukute, gatagata furuetemashita.*

★ I was really cold then, and I was shaking and rattling.

Small Steps

✲ 組織(そしき)がこわれかかっている様子(ようす)を表(あらわ)すこともある。

Also used to describe a broken organization.

例 今(いま)の監督(かんとく)に代(か)わって、チームが**ガタガタ**になった。

Ima no kantoku ni kawatte, chīmu ga gatagata ni natta.

The team has been in shambles after changing to the current manager.

不安定 Uncertainty

31 うろうろ

Urouro

25

行く方向や場所がはっきりせず、あちこち歩きまわる様子。

To wander here and there with no certain destination.

うろうろする、うろうろV「歩き回る」

Point 動く範囲はあまり広くない場合が多い。

Often used in situations where one does not have a wide range of movement.

---

1 Ⓐ ごはん、まだー？　おなか、すいた。

Ⓑ じゃまだから、台所を**うろうろ**しないで。もう、できるから。

Ⓐ *Gohan, madā? Onaka, suita.*

Ⓑ *Jama dakara, daidokoro o urouro shinaide. Mō, dekiru kara.*

Ⓐ Is dinner not ready yet? I'm hungry.

Ⓑ You're in the way, stop loitering around the kitchen. It'll be ready soon.

---

2 Ⓐ すみません、お待たせして。入口がわからなくて、**うろうろ**してしまいました。

Ⓑ いえいえ。ここ、ちょっとわかりにくいですよね。

Ⓐ *Sumimasen, omatase shite. Iriguchi ga wakaranakute, urouro shite shimaimashita.*

Ⓑ *Ieie. Koko, chotto wakari nikui desu yo ne.*

Ⓐ Sorry to make you wait. I didn't know where the entrance was and ended up loitering around.

Ⓑ Not at all. This area is a little hard to figure out.

32

キョロキョロ

{Glancing} Restlessly

Kyorokyoro

落ち着きなく、あたりを見回す様子。

To look around restlessly.

キョロキョロする、キョロキョロV「周りを見る」

Point 初めての場所に来たとき、何かを探しているときなどによく使う。

Often used when coming to a place for the first time or when looking for something.

---

1 Ⓐ どうしたの、**キョロキョロ**して。
Ⓑ どこかにコンビニがないかなあと思って。

Ⓐ *Dōshita no, kyorokyoro shite.*
Ⓑ *Dokoka ni konbini ga nai kanā tō omotte.*

Ⓐ What's the matter? Why are you glancing around restlessly?
Ⓑ I was wondering if there was a convenience store around here.

---

2 ★ こんな高級ホテルに入るのは初めてだから、つい、**キョロキョロ**しちゃう。

★ *Konna kōkyū hoteru ni hairu no wa hajimete dakara, tsui, kyorokyoro shichau.*

★ It's my first time in such a luxury hotel that I can't help but glance around restlessly.

33

26

グラグラ

Guragura

Unsteadily

物(もの)が安定(あんてい)せず、大(おお)きく揺(ゆ)れる様子(ようす)。

For something to not be stable and to waver greatly.

Typical forms グラグラする、グラグラV「揺(ゆ)れる」

Point 固定(こてい)されていたものが、ゆるくなっているときによく使(つか)う。

Often used when something that was once fixed is now slack.

1 Ⓐ どうしましたか。
Ⓑ ここの歯(は)がグラグラするんです。

Ⓐ *Dō shimashita ka?*
Ⓑ *Koko no ha ga guragura suru n desu.*

Ⓐ Is something the matter?
Ⓑ My tooth her feels unsteady.

2 Ⓐ この棚(たな)、ぐらぐらしてる。大丈夫(だいじょうぶ)かなあ。
Ⓑ ああ…ねじがはずれてるよ。

Ⓐ *Kono tana, guragura shiteru. Daijōbu kanā.*
Ⓑ *Ā…neji ga hazureteru yo.*

Ⓐ This shelf is unsteady. I wonder if it's okay.
Ⓑ Oh... A screw is loose.

Small Steps

例 会社(かいしゃ)やめようかどうしようか、グラグラしている。（気持(きも)ちが揺(ゆ)れている）

Kaisha yameyō ka dō shiyō ka, guragura shite iru.

I'm wavering on whether or not to quit my job. (One's feelings are swaying)

34

ゆらゆら

Yurayura

Waveringly

物(もの)がゆっくり大(おお)きく、くり返(かえ)し揺(ゆ)れている様子(ようす)。

For things to shake back and forth in a slow and large way.

ゆらゆらV「揺(ゆ)れる」、**ゆらゆらする、ゆらゆらとV**

Point 大(おお)きな力(ちから)を受(う)けて揺(ゆ)れているものについて言(い)う。

Used when describing something that is shaking due to a strong force.

---

1 Ⓐ 波(なみ)が高(たか)いから船(ふね)が**ゆらゆら**するよ、きっと。
Ⓑ そうだね。

Ⓐ *Nami ga takai kara fune ga yurayura suru yo, kitto.*
Ⓑ *Sō da ne.*

Ⓐ The waves are high, so the ships will probably waver.
Ⓑ You're right.

---

2 ★ 余震(よしん)でまだ**ゆらゆら**揺(ゆ)れているから気(き)をつけて。

★ *Yoshin de mada yurayura yurete iru kara ki o tsukete.*

★ Please be careful, aftershocks are still causing things to waver.

35

27

ふらふら

Furafura

Shakily

揺(ゆ)れ動(うご)いて安定(あんてい)していない様子(ようす)。

For something to not be stable as it wavers.

ふらふらする、ふらふらとV

Point 体(からだ)に力(ちから)が入(はい)らず、ふつうに立(た)ったり歩(ある)いたりできないときによく使(つか)う。

Often used when one's body is weak and unable to stand or walk normally.

1
Ⓐ まだ熱(ねつ)があるんじゃない？
Ⓑ うん。体(からだ)がちょっと**ふらふら**する。

Ⓐ *Mada netsu ga aru n ja nai?*
Ⓑ *Un. Karada ga chotto furafura suru.*

Ⓐ Don't you still have a fever?
Ⓑ Yes. My body still feels shaky.

2
Ⓐ 3時間(じかん)くらい歩(ある)いたかなあ。疲(つか)れたね。
Ⓑ もう、**ふらふら**だよ。朝(あさ)からまだ何(なに)も食(た)べてないし。

Ⓐ *San-jikan kurai aruita kanā. Tsukareta ne.*
Ⓑ *Mō, furafura dayo. Asa kara mada nani mo tabete nai shi.*

Ⓐ I guess we walked about three hours? Good work.
Ⓑ Phew, I'm feeling shaky. I haven't eaten anything since this morning, either.

✲ 行動(こうどう)や生活(せいかつ)が不安定(ふあんてい)な状態(じょうたい)を表(あらわ)すこともある。

Also used to describe uncertainty in actions or life.

例 卒業後(そつぎょうご)、**ふらふらしていた**時期(じき)もありました。

Sotsugyō go, furafura shite ita jiki mo arimashita.

There was a time when I was floating around after graduation.

36

ぶらぶら
Burabura

Dangling; idly

①ぶら下がったものが揺れ動く様子。
②目的がないまま行動したり生活したりする様子。

① For something dangling to shake back and forth
② To act or live without any goal.

Typical forms ぶらぶらする、ぶらぶらV「歩く」、ぶらぶらとV

Point 主に「ぶらぶらする」「ぶらぶらさせる」など動詞の形で使う。
Primarily used in verb forms such as「ぶらぶらする」or「ぶらぶらさせる」.

---

1 ★〈スポーツジムで〉では次に、両手を**ぶらぶら**させてください。

★ *[Supōtsu jimu de] Dewa tsugi ni, ryōte o burabura sasete kudasai.*

★ (At a sports gym) So next, dangle both your arms to the side.

---

2 Ⓐ どこにいたんですか。
Ⓑ ちょっと時間があったから、公園を**ぶらぶら**していました。

Ⓐ *Doko ni ita n desu ka?*
Ⓑ *Chotto jikan gātta kara, kōen o burabura shite imashita.*

Ⓐ Where did you go?
Ⓑ I had some time, so I spent it idly in the park.

隠れて　Hiding

37　28

ひそひそ
Hisohiso

Whisper

周りに聞こえないように小さな声で話す様子。
It seems like speaking in a small voice so that other people can not hear it.

Typical forms **ひそひそV**「話す」「言う」「悪口を言う」、**ひそひそとV**、**ひそひそ話**

Point 主に、人に聞かれたくない話をするときに使う。
This is primarily used when speaking at times when you don't want others to hear.

---

1 Ⓐ なに、二人で**ひそひそ**話してるの？
Ⓑ 別に。なんでもないよ。

Ⓐ What are you two talking in whisper?
Ⓑ No, particularly. Alright.

Ⓐ *Nani, futari de hisohiso hanashiteru no?*
Ⓑ *Betsuni. Nandemo nai yo.*

---

2 ★ **ひそひそ**話さないで、言いたいことがあったら、言ってください。

★ Don't talk in whisper. And, if you have something to say, please say it.

★ *Hisohiso hanasanaide, ītai koto ga attara, itte kudasai.*

Small Steps

✲ 密か(な)　*hisoka (na)*：secret
例 **密かな**楽しみ　*hisokana tanoshimi*：secret fun

✲ 単に小さい声で話すときは「小声で（言う、話す）」と言う。
When simply speaking in a soft voice,「小声で（言う、話す）」is used.

38

こそこそ

Kosokoso

Secretly

人に知られないように陰で静かに何かをする様子。

To do something in the shadows so that others do not know.

こそこそV「話す」「言う」、**こそこそする、こそこそとV**

Point「ひそひそ」は声だけに使うが、「こそこそ」は隠したい行動全般に使う。

「ひそひそ」is only used to describe voices, but「こそこそ」is used to describe hidden actions in general.

---

1 Ⓐ そんなところで、何を**こそこそ**やってるの？

Ⓑ えっ？　何もしてないよ。

Ⓐ *Sonna tokoro de, nani o kosokoso yatteru no?*

Ⓑ *Ett? Nani mo shite nai yo.*

Ⓐ What are you doing secretly there?

Ⓑ What? I'm not doing anything.

---

2 Ⓐ あれ？　石川君がいないね。

Ⓑ 片づけがいやだから、**こそこそ**帰ったんだよ。勝手なんだから。

Ⓐ *Are? Ishikawa-kun ga inai ne.*

Ⓑ *Katazuke ga iya dakara, kosokoso kaetta n da yo. Katte nan dakara.*

Ⓐ Hm? Ishikawa-kun isn't here, is he?

Ⓑ He doesn't like cleaning up, so he snuck out and went home. How selfish.

その他 Other

39 29

イチャイチャ

Ichaicha

Flirting

互いに甘えたりふざけ合ったりする。

To be coquettish or playful with someone else.

Typical forms **イチャイチャする、イチャイチャとV**

Point うらやましい気持ちや非難の気持ちを込めて使うことが多い。

Often used in a jealous or critical way.

---

1 Ⓐ いいなあ、あの二人。あんなふうに**イチャイチャ**してみたい。

Ⓑ じゃ、早く恋人をつくったら？

Ⓐ *Īnā, ano futari. Anna fū nīchaicha shite mitai.*

Ⓑ *Ja, hayaku koibito o tsukuttara?*

Ⓐ It must be so nice to be one of those two, getting to flirt around with each other like that.

Ⓑ In that case, why don't you hurry up and find a girlfriend?

---

2 ★ 公園に行ったら、**イチャイチャ**しているカップルばかりだった。

★ *Kōen nīttara, ichaicha shite iru kappru bakari datta.*

★ I went to the park, but there was nothing but couples flirting there.

PART 3

ものの状態を表す・強調する
じょうたい あらわ きょうちょう

Indicating/Emphasizing the State of Something

水、油
みず あぶら
Water, Oil

触った感触、見た感じ
さわ かんしょく み かん
The feel and look of it

輝き
かがや
Shining

元の形を失う
もと かたち うしな
Losing an original shape

混乱
こんらん
Confusion

柔らかさ
やわ
Softness

つくり
Build

サイズ
Size

密度、程度
みつど ていど
Consistency, Degree

いっぱい
Full

多少
たしょう
Amount

密度
みつど
Density

限界
げんかい
Limit

温度
おんど
Heat

料理・味
りょうり あじ
Food, flavor

天気
てんき
Weather

余裕
よゆう
Room; margin

人の状態
ひと じょうたい
A person's state

体調
たいちょう
Physical condition

全部クリア
ぜんぶ
Everything cleared

程度
ていど
Degree

その他
た
Other

水、油 Water, Oil

1 びしょびしょ

30

びしょびしょ

Bishobisho

全体にひどく濡れて、水分を含んでいる様子。

Extremely wet overall, with water inside of something.

びしょびしょだ、びしょびしょにV「濡れる」「なる」
名詞「びしょ濡れ」

Point 不快な気持ちを込めて言う。
Used with feelings of displeasure.

---

1 Ⓐ わあ、どうしたの？
Ⓑ 途中で雨が降ってきて、**びしょびしょ**になっちゃって。

Ⓐ *Wā, dōshitano?*
Ⓑ *Tochū de ame ga futte kite, bishobisho ni nacchatte.*

Ⓐ Whoa, what happened?
Ⓑ It started raining in the middle and I got drenched.

---

2 ★ 公園の噴水が突然こわれて、**びしょびしょ**に濡れてしまいました。

★ *Kōen no funsui ga totsuzen kowarete, bishobisho ni nurete shimaimashita.*

★ The fountain at the park suddenly broke and I was drenched.

✲ びっしょり：「びしょびしょ」と基本的に同じ。水分を多く含むことを強調した表現。

This is basically the same as びしょびしょ. It's an expression used to emphasise a large amount of water.

例 ラクビーの試合が終わったら、汗で**びっしょり**だった。
Ragubī no shiai ga owattara ase de bisshori datta.
I was drenched in sweat after the rugby match.

2

ベトベト

Betobeto

Sticky

粘(ねば)り気(け)のあるものが、人(ひと)の体(からだ)や物(もの)に付(つ)いて、なかなか離(はな)れない状態(じょうたい)。
When something sticky is on a person or thing and is not coming off.

ベトベトだ、ベトベトにV、ベトベトとV

Point 粘(ねば)り気(け)や湿気(しっけ)の強(つよ)いものが不快(ふかい)に感(かん)じるときに使(つか)う。
Used when feeling displeasure at something that is very sticky or humid.

---

1 Ⓐ 汗(あせ)で服(ふく)が**ベトベト**して気持(きも)ち悪(わる)い。
Ⓑ 私(わたし)も。早(はや)く涼(すず)しい所(ところ)に入(はい)ろう。

Ⓐ *Ase de fuku ga betobeto shite kimochi warui.*
Ⓑ *Watashi mo. Hayaku suzushī tokoro ni hairō.*

Ⓐ My clothes are sticky with sweat and I feel gross.
Ⓑ Me too. Let's hurry up and go somewhere cool.

---

2 Ⓐ 服(ふく)にはちみつがついて、**ベトベト**になっちゃったよ。
Ⓑ ああ、そこ？ でも、洗(あら)えばすぐ落(お)ちるよ。

Ⓐ *Fuku ni hachimitsu ga tsuite, betobeto ni nacchatta yo.*
Ⓑ *Ā soko? Demo, araeba sugu ochiru yo.*

Ⓐ My clothes got honey on them and now they're sticky.
Ⓑ Oh, right there? But it should come out right away if you wash it.

Small Steps

✲ ベットリ：「ベトベト」と基本的(きほんてき)に同(おな)じ。粘(ねば)りを強調(きょうちょう)した表現(ひょうげん)。
Stuck: When I was repairing my car, oil got stuck on my clothes. It might not come out.

例 車(くるま)の修理(しゅうり)をしたら、服(ふく)に油(あぶら)が**ベットリ**。落(お)ちないかも。
Kuruma no shūri o shitara, fuku ni abura ga bettori. Ochinai kamo.
When I was repairing my car, oil got stuck on my clothes. It might not come out.

3

31

ぬるぬる
Nurunuru

Slippery

表面(ひょうめん)が、粘(ねば)り気(け)のある液体(えきたい)におおわれて、すべりやすい状態(じょうたい)。
The state of a surface being covered in a viscous liquid, making it easy to slip.

ぬるぬるV「すべる」、**ぬるぬるとV**

Point 粘(ねば)り気(け)のある液体(えきたい)に触(ふ)れて、不快(ふかい)に感(かん)じるときに使(つか)う。
Used when feeling displeasure after touching a sticky liquid.

---

1 Ⓐ あ、そこ気(き)をつけて！
Ⓑ わあ、**ぬるぬる**すべって危(あぶ)ないね。

Ⓐ *A, soko ki o tsukete!*
Ⓑ *Wā, nurunuru subette abunai ne.*

Ⓐ Oh, watch out!
Ⓑ Wow, it's slippery and dangerous.

---

2 ★ 手(て)にクリームをつけすぎて、**ぬるぬる**している。

★ *Te ni kurīmu o tsuke sugite, nurunuru shite iru.*

★ I put too much cream on my hands and now they're slippery.

4

ネバネバ

Nebaneba

Gooey

よく粘って、ものにつきやすい状態。
また、簡単に切ったり離したりしにくい状態。

The state of something that is highly viscous, causing it to easily stick to things. Also used to describe the state of something that is easily cut and separated.

ネバネバする、ネバネバとV

Point 粘り気のある食べ物について、よく言う。
Often used to describe a gooey food item.

---

1 Ⓐ これ、すごく**ネバネバ**していますね。
Ⓑ **ネバネバ**する野菜は健康にいいそうですよ。

Ⓐ *Kore, sugoku nebaneba shite imasu ne.*
Ⓑ *Nebaneba suru yasai wa kenkō ni ī sō desu yo.*

Ⓐ This is very gooey, isn't it?
Ⓑ I hear that gooey vegetables are good for your health.

---

2 ★ 納豆は**ネバネバ**しているから、ちょっと苦手です。

★ *Nattō wa nebaneba shite iru kara, chotto nigate desu.*

★ Natto is gooey, so I have a little trouble with it.

触った感触、見た感じ The feel and look of it

5

ざらざら

Coarse

Zarazara

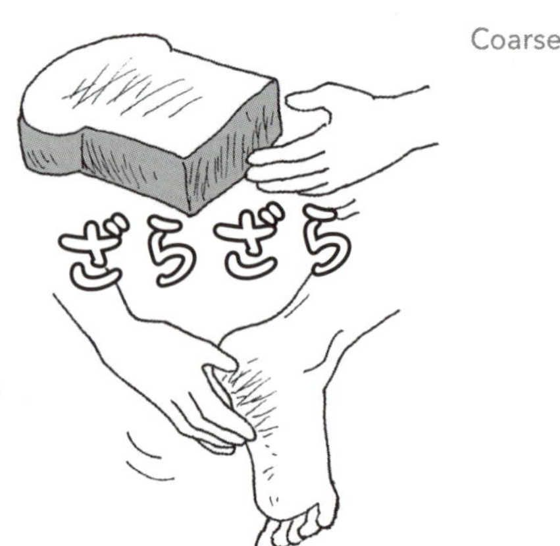

さわった感じがなめらかでなく、荒い様子。

Used to describe something that is rough and not smooth to the touch.

ざらざらする、ざらざらとV

Point 「すべすべ」や「つるつる」と反対。

The opposite of "slippery" or "smooth."

1 Ⓐ〈ソファー売り場〉こちらはいかがですか。
Ⓑ デザインは好きですが、表面が**ざらざら**してるのがちょっと…。

Ⓐ *[Sofā uriba] Kochira wa ikaga desu ka?*
Ⓑ *Dezain wa suki desu ga, hyōmen ga zarazara shiteru no ga chotto….*

Ⓐ (At a sofa sales floor) Would you like this one?
Ⓑ I like the design, but the fact that the surface is coarse is a little...

2 Ⓐ この名刺、いいですね。この、ちょっと**ざらざら**した紙がいいです。

Ⓐ *Kono mēshi ī desu ne. Kono, chotto zarazara shita kami ga ī desu.*

Ⓐ This is a nice business card. I like this slightly coarse paper.

6

すべすべ

Subesube

Slippery

さわった感(かん)じがなめらかで、好(この)ましい様子(ようす)。

Used to describe something that is favorably smooth to the touch.

Typical forms **すべすべする、すべすべのN**

Point 主(おも)にやわらかいものに対(たい)して使(つか)う。「ざらざら」などと反対(はんたい)の意味(いみ)。

Used primarily with soft objects. An antonym for terms like "coarse."

---

1 Ⓐ さくらさんの手(て)、**すべすべ**だね。何(なに)かつけてるの？
Ⓑ クリームをちょっとね。

Ⓐ *Sakura san no te, subesube dane. Nani ka tsuketeru no?*
Ⓑ *Kurīmu o chotto ne.*

Ⓐ Sakura-san, your hands are so slippery. What do you use on them?
Ⓑ A little bit of cream.

---

2 Ⓐ ここの温泉(おんせん)、肌(はだ)が**すべすべ**になるって。
Ⓑ いいねえ。楽(たの)しみ。

Ⓐ *Koko nōnsen, hada ga subesube ni narutte.*
Ⓑ *Ī nē. Tanoshimi.*

Ⓐ They say this hot spring makes your skin slippery.
Ⓑ That's great. I can't wait.

7

33

つやつや

Tsuyatsuya

Satiny

表面(ひょうめん)がなめらかで、光(ひかり)を受(う)けて輝(かがや)く様子(ようす)。

Used to describe something with a smooth surface that reflects light.

Point 髪(かみ)や肌(はだ)をほめるときに使(つか)うことが多(おお)い。

Often used to compliment hair and skin.

---

1 Ⓐ 髪(かみ)が**つやつや**で、うらやましいな。
Ⓑ 最近(さいきん)、ちょっといいシャンプーを使(つか)ってるんだ。

Ⓐ *Kami ga tsuyatsuya de, urayamashī na.*
Ⓑ *Saikin, chotto ī shanpū o tsukatteru n da.*

Ⓐ Your hair is so satiny, I'm jealous.
Ⓑ I've been using some kind of nice shampoo recently.

---

2 ★ この美容液(びようえき)を使(つか)うと、**つやつや**なお肌(はだ)になりますよ。

★ *Kono biyōeki o tsukau to, tsuyatsuya na ohada ni narimasu yo.*

★ Using this serum will give you satiny skin.

8

ツルツル

Tsurutsuru

Smooth

さわった感じがなめらかでつやがあり、すべりやすい様子。

Used to describe something that is smooth to the touch with a gloss to it that makes it slippery.

ツルツルする、ツルツルV「すべる」、ツルツルとV、ツルツルなN

Point 主に表面が硬いもの、水や油を含んだものに対して使う。
Primarily used when talking about hard surfaces and things that have water or oil in them.

---

1 Ⓐ この店のうどん、大好きなんだ。
Ⓑ わかる。麺が**ツルツル**だもんね。

Ⓐ *Kono mise no udon, daisuki nanda.*
Ⓑ *Wakaru. Men ga tsurutsuru damon ne.*

Ⓐ I love this store's udon.
Ⓑ I know what you mean. The noodles are so smooth.

---

2 ★ 雪道は**ツルツル**して滑りやすいから、気をつけて歩いてください。

★ *Yukimichi wa tsurutsuru shite suberi yasui kara, ki o tsukete aruite kudasai.*

★ Snowy roads are smooth and easy to slip on, so be careful when you walk on them.

9

34

しっとり

Shittori

Damp

①肌や髪、また、食べ物などに水分が十分ある様子。
②雰囲気などが、静かで落ち着いている様子。

① Used to describe skin, hair, or food that has a large amount of water content.
② Used to describe a quiet and calm state.

しっとりする、しっとりとV

Point 髪や肌をほめるときに使うことが多い。②は男性をほめるときには使いにくい。

Often used to compliment hair or skin. ② is hard to use when complimenting a man.

---

1 Ⓐ え？　70歳に見えないです。お肌が**しっとり**していて、とてもきれいです。
Ⓑ いえ、いえ。

Ⓐ *E? Nanajussai ni mienai desu. Ohada ga shittori shite ite, totemo kirē desu.*
Ⓑ *Ie,ie.*

Ⓐ What? You don't look 70. You have moist skin and you're very pretty.
Ⓑ No, not at all.

---

2 Ⓐ どんな方ですか。
Ⓑ 着物がよく似合う、**しっとり**とした女性です。

Ⓐ *Donna kata desu ka?*
Ⓑ *Kimono ga yoku niau, shittori to shita josē desu.*

Ⓐ What kind of person is she?
Ⓑ She's a very composed person who looks good in a kimono.

10

さらさら

Sarasara

Silky

①物(もの)が、どこかで止(と)まったりたまったりせず、軽(かる)く流(なが)れる様子(ようす)。
②湿気(しっけ)や粘(ねば)り気(け)がなく、乾(かわ)いていることが好(この)ましい様子(ようす)。

① Used to describe things that flow easily rather than get stopped up.
② Used to describe a dry state in a favorable way because it is not humid or sticky.

Typical forms さらさらする、さらさらV「流(なが)れる」、さらさらとV、名詞(めいし)「サラサラ髪(がみ)」

Point 表面(ひょうめん)について言(い)う場合(ばあい)、「ベトベト」や「ざらざら」などが反対(はんたい)の語(ご)。
Used as an antonym for "sticky," "coarse," etc. when describing surfaces.

---

1 Ⓐ あ、川(かわ)が**さらさら**流(なが)れてるね。
Ⓑ うん、水(みず)がきれい。魚(さかな)が泳(およ)いでるのがよく見(み)える。

Ⓐ Oh, the river is flowing there, isn't it?
Ⓑ Yes, ther water is creen. It's easy to see the fish swimming in it.

Ⓐ *A, kawa ga sarasara nagareteru ne.*
Ⓑ *Un, mizu ga kirē. Sakana ga oyoideru no ga yoku mieru.*

---

2 ★ シャンプーのモデルのように、髪(かみ)**さらさら**になりたい。

★ I want to have silky hair like a shampoo model's.

★ *Shanpū no moderu no yō ni, kami sarasara ni nari tai.*

11

パサパサ

Pasapasa

Dried

本来(ほんらい)あるべき水分(すいぶん)が失(うしな)われ、乾(かわ)いてしまっている状態(じょうたい)。

When something has lost its normal water content and is now dry.

Typical forms パサパサする、パサパサとV、名詞(めいし)「パサパサ髪(がみ)」

Point 乾燥(かんそう)した髪(かみ)や肌(はだ)によく使(つか)う。食(た)べ物(もの)については、水分(すいぶん)が抜(ぬ)けておいしくないことを表(あらわ)す。

Often used to describe dry hair or skin. Used to indicate food that has become dehydrated and is no longer tasty.

---

1 Ⓐ ちょっと。このパン、古(ふる)くない？
Ⓑ ほんとだ。**パサパサ**だね。

Ⓐ *Chotto. Kono pan, furuku nai?*
Ⓑ *Honto da. Pasapasa dane.*

Ⓐ Hold on. Isn't this bread old?
Ⓑ You're right. It's dry.

---

2 ★ ここは日本(にほん)と違(ちが)って、空気(くうき)が乾燥(かんそう)しているから、髪(かみ)が**パサパサ**になる。

★ *Koko wa nihon to chigatte, kūki ga kansō shite iru kara, kami ga pasapasa ni naru.*

★ Unlike Japan, the air is dry here so my hair is dried out.

輝き(かがや)き　Shining

12　35

ピカピカ

Pikapika

Shiny

表面(ひょうめん)が光(ひか)り輝(かがや)く様子(ようす)。

Used to describe a surface that shines with light.

ピカピカV「輝(かがや)く」「光(ひか)る」、ピカピカする、ピカピカとV

Point 新(あたら)しさや、汚(よご)れがなくきれいなことを表(あらわ)すときによく使(つか)う。

Often used to indicate something new or something that is pretty and not dirty.

1
Ⓐ 車(くるま)、**ピカピカ**ですね。
Ⓑ 今日(きょう)洗(あら)ったばかりなんです。

Ⓐ *Kuruma, pikapika desu ne.*
Ⓑ *Aratta bakari na n desu.*

Ⓐ The car is shiny and clean!
Ⓑ I've just cleaned it today.

2
★ あ、くつ、買ったんだ。**ピカピカ**だね。

★ *Att, kutsu katta n da. Pikapika da ne.*

★ Wow, you've bought some shoes. They're new and shiny, aren't they?

✻ 新(あたら)しさを強調(きょうちょう)する意味(いみ)でもよく使(つか)われる。

We often use this expression to emphasise how new something is.

例 **ピカピカ**の１年生(ねんせい)、**ピカピカ**の新品(しんぴん)

Pikapika no ichi-nensē, Pikapika no shinpin

shiny new first grader, brand new and shiny

13

キラキラ

Glittering

Kirakira

光を受けて輝いている様子。

Used to describe something that catches light and shines.

キラキラV「光る」「輝く」、キラキラする、キラキラとV
名詞「キラキラ星」「キラキラネーム」

Point 星や宝石、明かり、などについて言う。
Used with stars, gems, light, and so on.

---

1 Ⓐ 今夜は夜空がきれいだね。
Ⓑ そうだね。星が**キラキラ**している。

Ⓐ *Kon-ya wa yozora ga kirē dane.*
Ⓑ *Sō dane. Hoshi ga kirakira shite iru.*

Ⓐ The night sky is beautiful tonight, isn't it?
Ⓑ You're right. The stars are glittering.

---

2 ★ 選ばれた選手たちはみな**キラキラ**と目を輝かせた。

★ *Erabareta senshu tachi wa mina kirakira to me o kagayakaseta.*

★ The chosen athletes all had glittering eyes.

比ゆ的な表現もある。
Also used as a metaphorical expression.

例 彼、最近、大活躍だね。**キラキラ**してる。
Kare, saikin, daikatsuyaku dane. Kirakira shiteru.
He's been very busy lately. He's glittering.

元の形を失う　Losing an original shape

14

36

くしゃくしゃ

Kushakusha

Crumpled

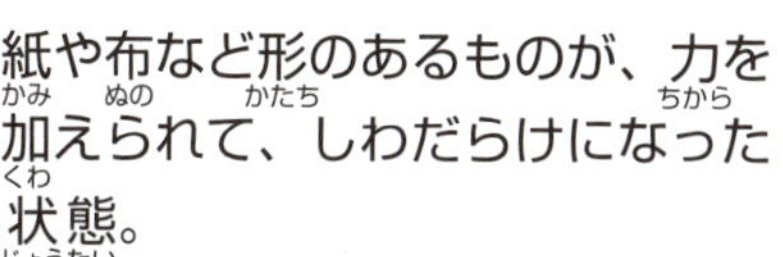

紙や布など形のあるものが、力を加えられて、しわだらけになった状態。

The state of something such as paper or cloth that had a shape becoming full of wrinkles after strength is applied to it.

くしゃくしゃだ、くしゃくしゃにV、くしゃくしゃのN

Point 全体的にしわがついてしまった状態。

The state of something being wrinkled all over.

---

1 Ⓐ あっ、その紙、捨てないで！
Ⓑ 遅いよ。もう**くしゃくしゃ**に丸めちゃった。

Ⓐ *Att, sono kami, sutenaide!*
Ⓑ *Osoi yo. Mō kushakusha ni marume chatta.*

Ⓐ Oh, don't throw that paper away!
Ⓑ Too late. I already crumpled it up in a ball.

---

2 ★ こんな**くしゃくしゃ**のシャツじゃお客さんに会えないよ。

★ *Konna kushakusha no shatsu ja okyakusan ni aenai yo.*

★ I can't meet customers with a shirt this crumpled.

15

ボロボロ

Boroboro

Tattered

傷んで破れたり、形が崩れたりしている状態。

For something to be injured and damaged, or for it to lose its shape.

Typical forms **ボロボロにV「なる」「する」、N がボロボロだ**

Point 布や皮などの状態について言うが、抽象的な事柄についても言う。

Used about the state of cloth and leather, but can also be used in abstract situations.

---

1 Ⓐ このじゅうたん、そろそろ取り替えない？
Ⓑ そうだね。この辺なんか、**ボロボロ**だもんね。

Ⓐ *Kono jūtan, sorosoro torikae nai?*
Ⓑ *Sō dane. Kono hen nanka, boroboro damon ne.*

Ⓐ Isn't it about time to change out this rug?
Ⓑ You're right. This part is tattered, even.

---

2 Ⓐ 最近、ずっと忙しそうですね。
Ⓑ うん、もう体が**ボロボロ**だよ。

Ⓐ *Saikin, zutto isogashi sō desu ne.*
Ⓑ *Un, mō karada ga boroboro da yo.*

Ⓐ You always seem busy lately.
Ⓑ Yes, my body is in tatters.

Small Steps

✲ 心の状態についても言う。

Also used to talk about a metal state.

例 彼に裏切られて、もう、心が**ボロボロ**です。

Kare ni uragirarete, mō, kokoro ga boroboro desu.

My heart is in tatters after being betrayed by him.

16

バラバラ
Barabara

Scattered

まとまっていたものや一つだったものが、割れたり離れたりして、別々になった状態。

For something that was together or as one to become broken apart and separated.

バラバラだ、バラバラにV、N がバラバラだ

Point 元々一つだったものや、一つになるべきものについて言う。

Used to talk about something that was once one, or that should be one.

---

1 Ⓐ このバイク、**バラバラ**にするから手伝って。
Ⓑ はい。

Ⓐ *Kono baiku, barabara ni suru kara tetsudatte.*
Ⓑ *Hai.*

Ⓐ I'm going to disassemble this bike, help me out.
Ⓑ Okay.

---

2 ★ 話し合ったけど、みんな意見が**バラバラ**で、まとまらなかった。

★ *Hanashi atta kedo, minna iken ga barabara de, matomara nakatta.*

★ We talked, but everyone's opinions were scattered and could not come together.

混乱 Confusion

17 37

ぐちゃぐちゃ

Guchagucha

Mushy

①水分を含んだものがつぶされたときの状態。
②整理が全くされず、ひどく乱れている状態。

① For something with water content to be crushed.
② For something to not come together at all and be horribly out of order.

ぐちゃぐちゃだ、ぐちゃぐちゃする、ぐちゃぐちゃにV

Point つぶれて、形がすっかり崩れた状態。

The state of something being crushed, causing its shape to be completely destroyed.

---

1 Ⓐ あっ、トマト落としちゃった！
Ⓑ わあ。ぐちゃぐちゃになっちゃったね。

Ⓐ *Att, tomato otoshichatta!*
Ⓑ *Wā. Guchagucha ni nacchatta ne.*

Ⓐ Oh, I dropped a tomato!
Ⓑ Ah, it's all mushy now.

---

2 Ⓐ 週末、遊びに行ってもいい？
Ⓑ だめ、だめ。今、引っ越しの準備してて、部屋がぐちゃぐちゃなのよ。

Ⓐ *Shūmatsu, asobi ni ittemo ī?*
Ⓑ *Dame, dame. Ima, hikkoshi no junbi shitete, heya ga guchagucha nano yo.*

Ⓐ Can I go over to play for a weekend?
Ⓑ No, no. I'm working on moving right now, so my room is a mess.

✲ 抽象的なことについても言う。 Also said about abstract matters.

例 彼が余計なことを言うから、話がぐちゃぐちゃになったよ。
Kare ga yokēna koto o iu kara, hanashi ga guchagucha ni natta yo.
He says unnecessary things, causing the conversation to become a mess.

18

めちゃくちゃ／めちゃめちゃ

Messed up; super

→p.158

Mechakucha /Mechamecha

①どうにもならないほどこわれた状態(じょうたい)や混乱(こんらん)した状態(じょうたい)。

②程度(ていど)が激(はげ)しいことを表(あらわ)す。

① For something to be so broken or disordered that nothing can be done about it.

② For something to be extreme in degree.

めちゃくちゃだ、めちゃくちゃにV、めちゃくちゃなN、めっちゃ Adj

Point ②は良(よ)いことにも、悪(わる)いことにも使(つか)う。

② is used for both good things and bad.

---

1 Ⓐ えーっ、そんな**めちゃくちゃ**な話(はなし)はないですよ。

Ⓑ ほんと、ひどいよね。

Ⓐ *Ētt, sonna mechakuchana hanashi wa nai desu yo.*

Ⓑ *Honto, hidoi yo ne.*

Ⓐ What? That's so messed up to hear.

Ⓑ Really, isn't it awful?

---

2 ★ 昨日(きのう)、パンダを見(み)に行(い)ったんだけど、**めちゃくちゃ**かわいかった。

★ *Kinō, panda o mi ni itta n da kedo, mechakucha kawaikatta.*

★ I went to see the pandas yesterday, but they were super cute.

✲「めっちゃ」の形(かたち)もよく使(つか)われる。 Also used in the form「めっちゃ」.

例 その漫画(まんが)、**めっちゃ**面白(おもしろ)いよ。

Sono manga, meccha omoshiroi yo.

That manga is super interesting.

19

ごちゃごちゃ

Gochagocha

Messy

多くのものが秩序なく混ざっている様子。

For many things to be mixed in a disordered way.

Typical forms **ごちゃごちゃする、ごちゃごちゃにV**

Point 異なるものが混じって、わかりにくい状態になっているときに使う。

Used when different things are mixed together, making them difficult to understand.

---

1 Ⓐ この本棚、古いのと新しいのが**ごちゃごちゃ**になってるね。
Ⓑ すみません。

Ⓐ *Kono hondana, furui no to atarashī no ga gochagocha ni natteru ne.*
Ⓑ *Sumimasen.*

Ⓐ This bookshelf has a mess of old and new books together.
Ⓑ I'm sorry.

---

2 ★ この辺は、店は多いし、道はせまいし、**ごちゃごちゃ**してますね。

★ *Kono hen wa, mise wa ōi shi, michi wa semai shi, gochagocha shite masu ne.*

★ This area has a lot of stores and narrow streets, it's so messy.

Small Steps

✲「文句を言う、不満を言う」などの意味もある。

Can also mean "To complain, to state dissatisfaction."

例 もう、わかったから、**ごちゃごちゃ**言わないで。(不平を言う)

Mō, wakatta kara, gochagocha iwanaide.(fufē o iu)

I get it, so just stop complaining (expressing displeasure).

柔(やわ)らかさ　Softness

20　38

ふわふわ

Fuwafuwa

Lightly

ふわふわ

①柔(やわ)らかく、ふくらんだ様子(ようす)。
① For something to be soft and puffed up.

②軽(かる)く漂(ただよ)う様子(ようす)。
② For something to float lightly.

Typical forms　**ふわふわV**「浮(う)かぶ」「揺(ゆ)れる」、**ふわふわとV**、**ふわふわのN**

Point さわった感(かん)じを表(あらわ)すときもあれば、見(み)た印象(いんしょう)を表(あらわ)すときもある。
Used to describe both the sensation of touch as well as visual impressions.

1
Ⓐ このオムレツ、**ふわふわ**！
Ⓑ ほんとだ。すごく柔(やわ)らかい。

Ⓐ *Kono omuretsu, fuwafuwa!*
Ⓑ *Honto da. Sugoku yawarakai.*

Ⓐ This omelet is so fluffy!
Ⓑ You're right. It's very soft.

2
★ 黒(くろ)い物(もの)が、海(うみ)に**ふわふわ**浮(う)かんでいた。
★ *Kuroi mono ga, umi ni fuwafuwa ukande ita.*

★ The black object floated in the sea airily.

Small Steps

✲ 落(お)ち着(つ)きがなく、軽(かる)く、いい加減(かげん)な様子(ようす)も表(あらわ)す。
Also used to describe something that does not calm down and is frivolous and irresponsible.

例 そんな**ふわふわ**した気持(きも)ちじゃ、この仕事(しごと)はできないよ。
Sonna fuwafuwa shita kimochi ja, kono shigoto wa dekinai yo.
You won't be able to do this work if you act that frivolously.

21

ふかふか

Fukafuka

Fluffy

柔(やわ)らかく膨(ふく)らんで、押(お)すと元(もと)に戻(もど)る様子(ようす)。

To be lightly swollen, and to return to an original shape if pressed.

ふかふかだ、ふかふかとV、ふかふかのN

Point ベッドやふとん、ソファーなどに使(つか)うのが典型的(てんけいてき)な例(れい)。

Most typically used with beds, futons, sofas, and so on.

---

1 Ⓐ わあ、気持(きも)ちいい、布団(ふとん)**ふかふか**だ。
Ⓑ そうでしょ？　今日(きょう)、布団(ふとん)干(ほ)したから。

Ⓐ *Wā, kimochi ī, futon fukafuka da.*
Ⓑ *Sō desho? Kyō, futon hoshita kara.*

Ⓐ Ooh, this feels so good. The futon is so fluffy.
Ⓑ Isn't it? I put it out to hang today.

---

2 ★ こんな**ふかふか**のソファーに座(すわ)ってると、眠(ねむ)くなっちゃう。

★ *Konna fukafuka no sofā ni suwatteru to, nemuku nacchau.*

★ I'm going to get sleepy sitting on a sofa this fluffy.

つくり Build

22

39

ほっそり
Hossori

Slender

細く、体の線がきれいに見える様子。

To be thin, to have a beautiful looking body shape.

ほっそりV「やせる」、ほっそりする、ほっそりとV

Point 手足や指など、体の一部にも使うことができる。
Can also be used for individual body parts such as limbs and fingers.

---

1 Ⓐ あの**ほっそり**した女性があなたのお姉さん？
Ⓑ ちがう、ちがう。姉はとなりの太いほう。

Ⓐ *Ano hossori shita josē ga anata no onēsan?*
Ⓑ *Chigau, chigau. Ane wa tonari no futoi hō.*

Ⓐ Is that slender woman your older sister?
Ⓑ No, no. My older sister is the fatter one next to her.

---

2 Ⓐ ダイエット頑張って５キロやせたよ。
Ⓑ ほんとだ。だいぶ**ほっそり**したね。

Ⓐ *Daietto ganbatte go kiro yaseta yo.*
Ⓑ *Honto da. Daibu hossori shita ne.*

Ⓐ I dieted hard and lost 5 kilograms.
Ⓑ You really did. You look a lot more slender.

23

ぽっちゃり

Pocchari

Chubby

体(からだ)に柔(やわ)らかさと丸(まる)みがあり、かわいらしい様子(ようす)。

To have a soft and round body that looks cute.

ぽっちゃりV「太(ふと)る」、ぽっちゃりする、ぽっちゃりとV

Point 太(ふと)っていることを間接的(かんせつてき)に言(い)うときにも使(つか)う。太(ふと)った体型(たいけい)を好意的(こういてき)に表(あらわ)す表現(ひょうげん)だが、失礼(しつれい)に感(かん)じる人(ひと)もいる。

Also used to indirectly say that someone or something is fat. While this is an expression that describes a fat body in a positive way, some people may find it rude.

---

1 Ⓐ だいぶ太(ふと)っちゃって恥(は)ずかしい。
Ⓑ そんなことないよ。**ぽっちゃり**してかわいいよ。

Ⓐ *Daibu futocchatte hazukashī.*
Ⓑ *Sonna koto nai yo. Pocchari shite kawaī yo.*

Ⓐ It's embarrassing that I got quite fat.
Ⓑ That's not true. You're chubby and cute.

---

2 ★ 子(こ)どもは**ぽっちゃり**しているほうが病気(びょうき)しないらしい。

★ *Kodomo wa pocchari shite iru hō ga byōki shinai rashī.*

★ I hear that children are less likely to get sick if they're chubby.

24

がっしり

Gasshiri

Solid

人の体や物のつくりが力強く、安定している様子。

For the build of a person or object to be strong and sturdy.

がっしりV「する」「です」、**がっしりとV**

Point 人の体や家具、建物などによく使う。

Often used to describe people's bodies, or furniture, buildings, and so on.

---

1 Ⓐ 彼、ラグビーやってたんだって。

Ⓑ なるほど。それで、体が**がっしり**してるんだ。

Ⓐ *Kare, ragubī yatteta n datte.*

Ⓑ *Naruhodo. Sore de, karada ga gasshiri shiteru n da.*

Ⓐ He says he used to play rugby.

Ⓑ That makes sense. So that's why he has such a solid body.

---

2 Ⓐ 荷物、このテーブルの上に置いて大丈夫？　かなり重いけど。

Ⓑ 大丈夫だよ。そのテーブル、結構**がっしり**してるから。

Ⓐ *Nimotsu, kono tēburu no ue ni oite daijōbu? Kanari omoi kedo.*

Ⓑ *Daijōbu dayo. Sono tēburu, kekkō gasshiri shiteru kara.*

Ⓐ Can I put my baggage on top of this table? It's pretty heavy.

Ⓑ It's fine, that table is pretty solid.

サイズ Size

25

だぶだぶ

Dabudabu

Loose

服(ふく)が大(おお)きすぎて、ゆるんでいる様子(ようす)。

For clothes to be too big that they are baggy.

だぶだぶだ、だぶだぶのN、だぶだぶなN

Point 服(ふく)、ズボン、セーター、スーツなどが一緒(いっしょ)によく使(つか)われる。

Often used in conjunction with clothes, pants, sweaters, suits, and so on.

1

Ⓐ さっきのズボンはだめだったの？

Ⓑ うん。履(は)いてみたら、**だぶだぶ**だった。

Ⓐ *Sakki no zubon wa dame datta no?*

Ⓑ *Un. Haite mitara, dabudabu datta.*

Ⓐ Were those pants earlier no good?

Ⓑ Yeah. I tried wearing them but they were loose.

2

★ 太(ふと)っていた頃(ころ)のジャケットは**だぶだぶ**で、今(いま)では着(き)られない。

★ *Futotte ita koro no jaketto wa dabudabu de, ima dewa kirare nai.*

★ The jacket from when I was fat is loose, so I can't wear it now.

26

ぶかぶか

Bukabuka

Baggy

くつや帽子(ぼうし)などが大(おお)きすぎて、余(あま)っている様子(ようす)。

For shoes, a hat, or so on to be so big that there is extra space.

Typical forms ぶかぶかだ、ぶかぶかのN、ぶかぶかなN

Point くつや帽子(ぼうし)、ズボンなどが一緒(いっしょ)によく使(つか)われる。

Most often used in conjunction with shoes, hats, pants, and so on.

---

1 Ⓐ ダイエットしたら、靴(くつ)まで**ぶかぶか**になっちゃった。
Ⓑ えっそうなの？

Ⓐ *Daietto shitara, kutsu made bukabuka ni nacchatta.*
Ⓑ *Ett sō na no?*

Ⓐ After going on a diet, even my shoes were baggy.
Ⓑ What, really?

---

2 ★ 兄(あに)に帽子(ぼうし)をもらったんだけど、**ぶかぶか**で使(つか)えなかった。

★ *Ani ni bōshi o moratta n da kedo, bukabuka de tsukae nakatta.*

★ I got a hat from my older brother, but it was baggy and I couldn't use it.

27

41

キツキツ

Kitsukitsu

Tight

①服(ふく)やくつなどのサイズが小(ちい)さすぎる様子(ようす)。
②空間(くうかん)がせますぎる様子(ようす)。

① For clothes, shoes, and so on to be too small in size.
② For a space to be too cramped.

キツキツだ、キツキツなN、キツキツのN

Point 小(ちい)さすぎたり狭(せま)すぎたりして、非常(ひじょう)に窮屈(きゅうくつ)なこと。
Used to describe extreme tightness due to something being too small or narrow.

---

1 Ⓐ この制服(せいふく)、小(ちい)さすぎて、**キツキツ**です。
Ⓑ そうですか、じゃ取(と)り替(か)えましょう。

Ⓐ *Kono sēfuku, chīsasugite, kitsukitsu desu.*
Ⓑ *Sō desuka, ja torikae mashō.*

Ⓐ This uniform is too small, and it's tight.
Ⓑ Is that so. Then let me exchange it for you.

---

2 Ⓐ この本(ほん)も棚(たな)に置(お)ける？
Ⓑ **キツキツ**だけど、何(なん)とか。

Ⓐ *Kono hon mo tana ni okeru?*
Ⓑ *Kitsukitsu da kedo, nantoka.*

Ⓐ Can you put this book on the shelf, too?
Ⓑ It's tight, but I think I can manage.

28

ぴったり
Pittari

Perfect

サイズやセンスがちょうど合(あ)う様子(ようす)。

For the size or sense of something to be just right.

Typical forms **ぴったりだ、ぴったりV「合(あ)う」**

Point 違(ちが)うところ、ずれているところが全(まった)くないこと。

For there to be nothing wrong or off.

---

1 Ⓐ これ、プレゼント。受(う)け取(と)って。
Ⓑ ありがとう。わあ、サイズ**ぴったり**。

Ⓐ *Kore, purezento. Uketotte.*
Ⓑ *Arigatō. Wā, saizu pittari.*

Ⓐ This is a present. Please take it.
Ⓑ Thank you. Wow, the size is perfect.

---

2 Ⓐ あの二人(ふたり)は息(いき)が**ぴったり**合(あ)ってるね。
Ⓑ うん。あんなふうに踊(おど)れたら、かっこいいね。

Ⓐ *Ano futari wa iki ga pittari atteru ne.*
Ⓑ *Un. Anna fū ni odoretara, kakkoī ne.*

Ⓐ Those two are perfectly in synch.
Ⓑ Yes. It would be so cool if you could dance like that.

密度、程度 Consistency, Degree

29

42

がらがら

Garagara

Empty

ある場所に人がほとんどいなくて、空いた空間が目立つ様子。

For barely anyone to be in a location that is notable when empty.

Nはがらがらだ

Point 客が少ないことを表すときによく使う。

Often used when there are few customers in a location.

---

1 Ⓐ すいてるね、映画館。

Ⓑ ほんと。週末は混んでるのに、平日は**がらがら**だね。

Ⓐ *Suiteru ne, ēgakan.*

Ⓑ *Honto. Shūmatsu wa konderu noni, hējitsu wa garagara da ne.*

Ⓐ There aren't many people at this movie theater, are there?

Ⓑ There really aren't. It's so crowded on the weekends, but I guess it's empty on the weekdays.

---

2 ★ お正月は東京も**がらがら**になるね。

★ *Oshōgatsu wa tōkyō mo garagara ni naru ne.*

★ Even Tokyo is empty during New Year's.

30

すかすか

Sukasuka

Flimsy

ある範囲の中にすき間が多くある状態。中身が乏しい状態。

For there to be many holes across a certain range. Used when the content of something is meager.

Nはすかすかだ

Point 中身が充実していないことへの不満を表すときによく使う。

Often used when expressing dissatisfaction that the content of something is not substantial.

---

1 Ⓐ 箱は大きいけど、中は**すかすか**なんじゃない？
Ⓑ きっと高いものが入ってるんじゃない？

Ⓐ *Hako wa ōkī kedo, naka wa sukasuka nan ja nai?*
Ⓑ *Kitto takai mono ga haitteru n ja nai?*

Ⓐ The box is big, but isn't it hollow inside?
Ⓑ There's probably something expensive inside, no?

---

2 ★ このサンドイッチ、**すかすか**。買って損した。

★ *Kono sandoicchi, sukasuka. Katte son shita.*

★ There's nothing much in this sandwich. I shouldn't have bought it.

いっぱい Full

31

43

ぎっしり

Gisshiri

Packed

中身が隙間なく詰まっていて重い状態。
For something to be packed to the point that it is heavy with no extra space inside of it.

Nはぎっしりだ

Point 立体的なイメージ。人についても使う。
Gives a three-dimensional image. Also used about people.

---

1 Ⓐ すごい弁当だね。ご飯が**ぎっしり**！
Ⓑ そう？　これぐらい食べないと、力が出ないよ。

Ⓐ *Sugoi bentō da ne. Gohan ga gisshiri!*
Ⓑ *Sō? Kore gurai tabenai to, chikara ga denai yo.*

Ⓐ What a boxed lunch. It's packed full of rice!
Ⓑ Really? I don't have any strength unless I eat about this much.

---

2 ★ 来月は予定が**ぎっしり**で、旅行に行くのは無理です。

★ *Raigetsu wa yotē ga gisshiri de, ryokō ni iku no wa muri desu.*

★ My weekend is packed with plans, so I can't go on a trip.

32

びっしり

Bisshiri

Close

物が詰まって隙間なく並んでいる状態。

For things to be lined up in a full way that results in no extra space.

Typical forms **Nはびっしりだ**

Point 平面的なイメージ。人については使わない。

Gives a flat image. Not used to describe people.

---

1 Ⓐ 明るいバスルームですね。
Ⓑ ええ、カラフルなタイルを壁に**びっしり**置きましたから。

Ⓐ *Akarui basurūmu desu ne.*
Ⓑ *Ē, karafuru na tairu o kabe ni bisshiri okimashita kara.*

Ⓐ What a bright bathroom.
Ⓑ Yes, it's because I put colorful tiles close to each other along the wall.

---

2 ★ 彼女は、いつもノートに**びっしり**書き込んでいます。

★ *Kanojo wa, itsumo nōto ni bisshiri kakikonde irmasu.*

★ She's always writing in her notebook and filling it up.

多少（たしょう） Amount

33

44

たっぷり
Tappuri

Plenty

あふれるほどたくさんある様子（ようす）。

For there to be so much of something that it is abundant.

たっぷりV「ある」、たっぷりだ、たっぷりとV

Point 「時間（じかん）」「食（た）べ物（もの）」など、数（かぞ）えられない言葉（ことば）と一緒（いっしょ）に使（つか）う。

Used together with words that cannot be counted, such as time or food.

1

Ⓐ 歓迎会（かんげいかい）、どこでやろうか。
Ⓑ またバイキングの店（みせ）がいいな。**たっぷり**食（た）べられるし。

Ⓐ *Kangēkai, doko de yarō ka?*
Ⓑ *Mata baikingu no mise ga ī na. Tappuri taberareru shi.*

Ⓐ Where should we hold the welcoming party?
Ⓑ Maybe another buffet. We'll be able to eat plenty that way, too.

2

★ 時間（じかん）は**たっぷり**ありますから、ゆっくり考（かんが）えてください。

★ *Jikan wa tappuri arimasu kara, yukkuri kangaete kudasai.*

★ I have plenty of time, so take your time and think about it.

Small Steps

例 彼（かれ）はいつも自信（じしん）**たっぷり**だね。
Kare wa itsumo jishin tappuri da ne.
He's always full of confidence.

34

ちょこっと

Chokotto

A bit

ほんの少しだけという意味。

A term that means just a small amount.

Typical forms ちょこっとだ、ちょこっとV「飲む」「やる」

Point「ちょっと」よりさらに少ないことを強調した表現。

An expression used to emphasize that there is even less of something than「ちょっと」.

---

1 Ⓐ 君はお酒のむの？
Ⓑ はい、**ちょこっと**ですけど。

Ⓐ *Kimi wa osake nomu no?*
Ⓑ *Hai, chokotto desu kedo.*

Ⓐ Do you drink alcohol?
Ⓑ Yes, but just a bit.

---

2 Ⓐ 彼はシャイですね。
Ⓑ そう。**ちょこっと**目を合わせて、すぐ下を向くんだよね。

Ⓐ *Kare wa shai desu ne.*
Ⓑ *Sō. Chokotto me o awasete, sugu shita o muku n da yo ne.*

Ⓐ He's shy, isn't he?
Ⓑ Yes. He looks down immediately even if you make a bit of eye contact.

Small Steps

✲ 例 日本語は**ちょこっと**だけ話せます。(謙遜表現)

Nihongo wa chokotto dake hanasemasu. (kenson hyōgen)

I only speak a bit of Japanese (Humble expression)

密度（みつど） Density

35 ぎゅっと

45

ぎゅっと

Gyutto

Squeezed

瞬間的に力を強く入れてしめたり握ったりすること。

To close or grip something by putting a large amount of force into it for a moment.

ぎゅっとV「しめる」「抱きしめる」

Point 「握る」「抱く」「抱きしめる」などと一緒に使うことが多い。

Often used together with terms like "grip," "hold," or "clasp."

---

1 Ⓐ 袋に中身を入れたら、口を**ぎゅっと**しめてね。

Ⓑ はい。

Ⓐ *Fukuro ni nakami o iretara, kuchi o gyutto shimete ne.*

Ⓑ *Hai.*

Ⓐ After putting it in the bag, close it tight.

Ⓑ Okay.

---

2 ★ この子供たちを**ぎゅっと**抱きしめてあげたい。

★ *Kono kodomo tachi o gyutto dakishimete agetai.*

★ I want to squeeze these kids and hug them.

36

ぎゅうぎゅう

gyūgyū

Packed

十分な空間がない所に、強く押して無理に入れる様子。

To push and force one's way into a place where there is not enough space.

Point くり返し強く押したり押されたりするときに使う。

Used when repeatedly pushing or being pushed with force.

---

1 Ⓐ 朝のラッシュアワーに電車乗りたくないね。

Ⓑ そうだね。駅員に**ぎゅうぎゅう**押し込まれるからね。

Ⓐ *Asa no rasshu awā ni densha noritaku nai ne.*

Ⓑ *Sō da ne. Ekiin ni gyūgyū oshikomareru kara ne.*

Ⓐ I don't want to get on a morning rush hour train.

Ⓑ You're right. You'll get pushed and packed in by station employees.

---

2 ★ そんなに服を**ぎゅうぎゅう**詰め込んだら、トランク壊れちゃうよ。

★ *Sonna ni fuku o gyūgyū tumekondara, toranku kowarechau yo.*

★ Packing your clothes that tight will break your suitcase, you know.

限界 Limit

37 ぎりぎり

Girigiri

46

Barely

あとほんの少しで限界になるという状態。

For something to nearly be at its limit.

ぎりぎりだ、ぎりぎりV「間に合う」

Point 時間的にも空間的にも使える。

Used to talk about both time and space.

---

1 Ⓐ **ぎりぎり**間に合ったね。
Ⓑ うん。でも、ほんと、焦ったよ。

Ⓐ *Girigiri ma ni atta ne.*
Ⓑ *Un. Demo, honto, asetta yo.*

Ⓐ We just barely made it.
Ⓑ Yes. But I really got nervous.

---

2 ★ 思ったよりお金がかかったので、予算**ぎりぎり**でした。

★ *Omotta yori okane ga kakatta node, yosan girigiri deshita.*

★ It cost more than I thought, so we were just barely within budget.

38

パンパン

Panpan

Jammed

物がいっぱいで、入れ物が破れそうなほど、ふくらんでいる様子。

For something to be so full that it is bulging to the point where the container seems like it will break.

Typical forms パンパンだ、パンパンにV「入っている」

Point カバンや袋など、主に柔らかい入れ物について使う。

It is used mainly to talk about something soft, like a handbag.

---

1 Ⓐ おいしいね。
Ⓑ いっぱい食べ過ぎて、お腹**パンパン**だよ。

Ⓐ *Oishī ne.*
Ⓑ *Ippai tabe sugite, onaka panpan da yo.*

Ⓐ This is delicious, isn't it?
Ⓑ I ate so much that my stomach is packed full.

---

2 ★ いろいろ入れるから、いつもカバンが**パンパン**だ。

★ *Iroiro ireru kara, itsumo kaban ga panpan da.*

★ I put so many things in my bag that it's always jam packed.

温度 Heat

39

47

ポカポカ
Pokapoka

Warm

温かくて気持ちがよいこと。
For something to be warm and comfortable.

ポカポカする、ポカポカと、ポカポカのN

Point 体が温まるときに使う。
Used when your body is warmed.

---

1 Ⓐ やっぱり温泉って気持ちいいね。
Ⓑ うん、出た後も体が**ポカポカ**するね。

Ⓐ *Yappari onsen tte kimochi ī ne.*
Ⓑ *Un, deta atomo karada ga pokapoka suru ne.*

Ⓐ Hot springs really do feel good.
Ⓑ Yes, and your body is warm after you get out.

---

2 Ⓐ 最近、ずっといい天気だね。寒くもないし、暑くもないし。
Ⓑ うん。**ポカポカ**して、眠くなるよ。

Ⓐ *Saikin, zutto ī tenki da ne. Samuku mo nai shi, atsuku mo nai shi.*
Ⓑ *Un. Pokapoka shite, nemuku naru yo.*

Ⓐ The weather's constantly been nice recently. It's not cold, and it's not hot.
Ⓑ Yes. I get sleepy from how warm it is.

40

アツアツ

Atsuatsu

Hot

① 料理(りょうり)したてでとても熱(あつ)い状態(じょうたい)。
② 男女(だんじょ)などが、とても強(つよ)く愛(あい)し合(あ)っている様子(ようす)。

① For something to be very hot just after being cooked.
② For two people to be very strongly in love with each other.

アツアツだ、アツアツのN

Point 最高(さいこう)に熱(あつ)い状態(じょうたい)を表(あらわ)す。
Used to describe something that is incredibly hot.

---

1 Ⓐ できたばかりで**アツアツ**だから、気(き)をつけてね。
Ⓑ うん。おいしそう。

Ⓐ *Dekita bakari de atsuatsu dakara, ki o tsukete ne.*
Ⓑ *Un. Oishisō.*

Ⓐ It's hot and fresh, be careful.
Ⓑ Okay. It looks good.

---

2 ★ あの二人(ふたり)、結婚(けっこん)して 20 年(ねん)たっても**アツアツ**でいいね。

★ *Ano futari, kekkon shite nijū-nen tattemo atsuatsu de ī ne.*

★ Those two are still in a hot relationship even though 20 years have passed since they were married.

41

ひんやり

Hin'yari

Chilly

冷たさが気持ちよく感じられる様子。
(つめ　きも　かん　ようす)

Describes a kind of coldness that feels good.

Typical forms **ひんやりする、ひんやりとV、ひんやりN**「グッズ」「枕(まくら)」「シーツ」「タオル」

Point 空気(くうき)や飲み物(のもの)について言う(い)ことが多い(おお)。
Often used to describe the air or drinks.

---

1 Ⓐ 外(そと)は暑(あつ)いけど、ビルに入(はい)ると**ひんやり**するね。
Ⓑ そうだね。

Ⓐ *Soto wa atsui kedo, biru ni hairu to hin'yari suru ne.*
Ⓑ *Sō da ne.*

Ⓐ It's hot out, but it's chilly inside this building.
Ⓑ You're right.

---

2 ★ 高原(こうげん)の朝(あさ)は、空気(くうき)が**ひんやり**して気持(きも)ちいい。

★ *Kōgen no asa wa, kūki ga hin'yari shite kimochiī.*

★ Mornings in the plains feel good with the chilly air.

料理・味　Food, flavor

42　　48

こってり

Kotteri

Rich

味が濃く、深みがあり、後によく残ること。

For something to have a strong, deep taste that lasts.

Typical forms　**こってりする、こってりとV、こってりN「味」**

Point スープの特徴を言うときなどによく使う。反対の言葉は「あっさり」。

Often used when describing a soup and so on. The antonym of this is「あっさり」.

1
Ⓐ ラーメンは、**こってり**した味が好きです。
Ⓑ じゃ、いい店、知ってるから、今度、行こうか。

Ⓐ *Rāmen wa, kotteri shita aji ga suki desu.*
Ⓑ *Ja, ī mise, shitteru kara, kondo, ikō ka.*

Ⓐ I like ramen that is rich in flavor.
Ⓑ Then I know a good store. Let's go together some time.

2
Ⓐ このスープは**こってり**して、おいしいですね。
Ⓑ そうですか。バターを少し入れたんです。

Ⓐ *Kono sūpu wa kotteri shite, oishī desu ne.*
Ⓑ *Sō desu ka. Batā o sukoshi ireta n desu.*

Ⓐ This soup is rich and tasty.
Ⓑ Is it? I put a little butter in it.

Small Steps

✲ 時間をかけて激しく叱る様子を表す。

Used to describe scolding someone harshly over a long amount of time.

例 ミスをして、部長に**こってり**怒られた。

Misu o shite, buchō ni kotteri okorareta.

I messed up, so the division chief got really mad at me.

43

あっさり

Assari

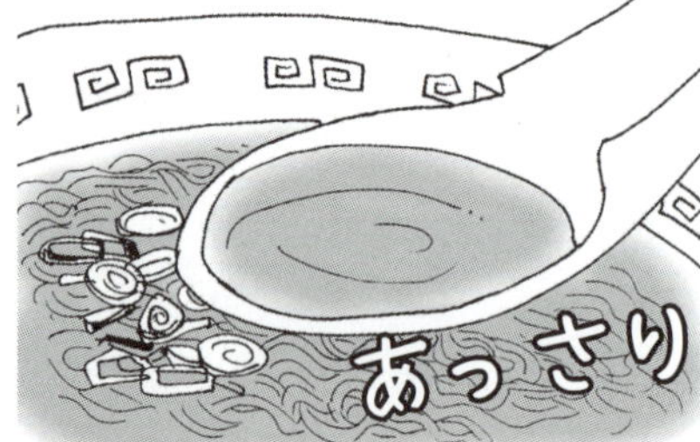

Light

味が薄めで、あまり後に残らないこと。

For something to have a thin taste that does not really stay behind.

あっさりする、あっさりV「みとめる」、**あっさりとV、あっさりN**「味」

Point 食べ物、人、デザインなどによく使われる。

Often used for food, people, designs, and more.

---

1 Ⓐ このスープ、**あっさり**してるね。
Ⓑ そうだね、見た目と違うね。

Ⓐ *Kono sūpu, assari shiteru ne.*
Ⓑ *Sō da ne, mitame to chigau ne.*

Ⓐ This is a light soup, isn't it?
Ⓑ You're right, it's not like it looks.

---

2 ★ 京都の料理って、**あっさり**した味付けが多いね。

★ *Kyōto no ryōri tte, assari shita ajitsuke ga ōi ne.*

★ Kyoto food often is seasoned in a light way, isn't it?

✲ 態度や行動にこだわりや複雑な面がない様子を表す。

Used to describe an attitude or action that does not have strong preferences or a complex side.

例 会議を欠席したいと部長にお願いしたら、**あっさり** OK してくれた。

Kaigi o kesseki shitai to buchō ni onegai shitara assari ōkē shite kureta.

When I asked the division chief if I could not attend the meeting, he gave me an easy OK.

44

49

さっぱり

→p.155、p.202

Simple

Sappari

味が、シンプルで、後に残らないこと。

For something to taste simple and not linger.

Typical forms さっぱりする、さっぱりとV、さっぱりN「味」

Point 味がしつこくないこと。

For a taste to not be too persistent.

1 Ⓐ お昼、何、食べる？
Ⓑ 暑いから、何か**さっぱり**したものがいいな。

Ⓐ *Ohiru, nani, taberu?*
Ⓑ *Atsui kara, nanika sappari shita mono ga ī na.*

Ⓐ What do you want to eat for lunch?
Ⓑ It's hot, so I think something simple would be good.

2 ★ 肉にレモン（汁）をかけると、**さっぱり**して、おいしいよ。

★ *Niku ni remon(jiru) o kakeru to, sappari shite, oishī yo.*

★ Putting lemon (juice) on meat makes it taste simple and delicious.

45

ピリッと

Prickle

Piritto

口に入れた途端、瞬間的に強い刺激を受ける様子。

To feel a momentary, strong stimulation when putting something in your mouth.

Typical forms ピリッとする、ピリッとV「くる」、ピリッと Adj「辛い」

Point「ピリッ」は、辛味や刺激を表す。

「ピリッ」expresses spiciness or stimulation.

---

1 Ⓐ あと、コショウをちょっと入れようか。
Ⓑ そうだね。**ピリッと**しておいしくなるよ、きっと。

Ⓐ *Ato, koshō o chotto ireyō ka.*
Ⓑ *Sō da ne. Piritto shite oishiku naru yo, kitto.*

Ⓐ Let's also put in a little bit of pepper.
Ⓑ That's right. The prickle will make it taste good, I think.

---

2 ★ こちらのスープはカレー味で、**ピリッと**辛いのが特徴です。

★ *Kochira no sūpu wa karē aji de, piritto karai no ga tokuchō desu.*

★ This soup is curry flavored, and it is notable for having a prickling spiciness.

Small Steps

意見や考え方が鋭いことを表す。
Used to describe pointed opinions or ways of thinking.

例 最後に**ピリッと**した意見を言ってくれて、ありがとう。
Saigo ni piritto shita iken o itte kurete, arigatō.
Thank you for giving that pointed opinion at the end.

46

50

コトコト

Kotokoto

Simmering

弱火(よわび)で時間(じかん)をかけて煮(に)るときの様子(ようす)。
To stew something over low heat for a long period of time.

Typical forms **コトコトV「煮(に)る」、コトコトとV**

Point 鍋(なべ)を使(つか)った料理(りょうり)によく使(つか)う。
Often used for foods cooked in a pot.

---

1 Ⓐ 何(なに)かおいしそうなにおいがするね。
Ⓑ うん、今(いま)、シチューを**コトコト**煮(に)てるから。

Ⓐ *Nanika oishisō na nioi ga suru ne.*
Ⓑ *Un, ima, shichū o kotokoto niteru kara.*

Ⓐ Something smells good.
Ⓑ Yes, some stew is simmering right now.

---

2 ★ 材料(ざいりょう)を入(い)れたら、あとは、1時間(じかん)くらい**コトコト**煮(に)るだけです。

★ *Zairyō o iretara ato wa, ichi jikan kurai kotokoto niru dake desu.*

★ After you put in the ingredients, all you have to do is let it simmer for about an hour.

47

がっつり

Gattsuri

Proper; heavy

好きなだけ、たくさん食べること。

To eat as much as one wants, or a large amount.

がっつりV「食べる」、**がっつりとV**

Point「たくさん、十分、しっかり」の意味。

A lot, plenty, a solid amount.

---

1 Ⓐ 今日はよく運動したから、お腹すいたでしょ？

Ⓑ うん。ステーキとか、**がっつり**食べたいね。

Ⓐ *Kyō wa yokūndo shita kara, onaka suita desho?*

Ⓑ *Un. Stēki toka, gattsuri tabetai ne.*

Ⓐ You worked out a lot today, you must be hungry.

Ⓑ Yes. I want to eat a proper meal, like a steak or something.

---

2 ★ 朝はそんなに食べません。その分、昼に**がっつり**食べます。

★ *Asa wa sonna ni tabemasen. Sono bun, hiru ni gattsuri tabemasu.*

★ I don't eat that much at breakfast. After that, I eat a large, proper lunch.

余裕(よゆう) Room; margin

48

51

Yukkuri

Steadily

動作(どうさ)が遅(おそ)い様子(ようす)。時間(じかん)や心(こころ)に余裕(よゆう)を持(も)って何(なに)かをする様子(ようす)。

For an action to proceed slowly. To do something while taking one's time or feeling like there is breathing room.

Typical forms **ゆっくりする、ゆっくりV「話(はな)す」「歩(ある)く」、ゆっくりとV**

Point スピードが遅(おそ)いこと。また、急(いそ)がないこと。

For something to be slow in speed. Also, to not rush.

---

1 Ⓐ 1212438です。
Ⓑ えっ、すみませんが、もう一度(いちど)**ゆっくり**言(い)ってください。

Ⓐ *Ichi ni ichi ni yon san hachi desu.*
Ⓑ *Ett, sumimasen ga, mō ichi do yukkuri itte kudasai.*

Ⓐ It's 1 2 1 2 4 3 8.
Ⓑ Um, sorry, but could you please repeat that slowly?

---

2 ★ ずっと忙(いそが)しかったから、温泉(おんせん)で**ゆっくり**しましょう。

★ *Zutto isogashikatta kara, onsen de yukkuri shimashō.*

★ I was busy for so long, I think I'll relax in a hot spring.

49

のんびり

Nonbiri

Relaxed

急(いそ)がず、リラックスして、ゆっくり何(なに)かをする様子(ようす)。

To do something without rushing while feeling relaxed in a steady way.

のんびりする、のんびりV「過(す)ごす」、のんびりとV

Point 急(いそ)がなければならない場面(ばめん)で否定的(ひていてき)に使(つか)うことも多(おお)い。

Often used negatively in situations where one needs to hurry.

1 Ⓐ ときどき、都会(とかい)を離(はな)れて**のんびり**したいですね。

Ⓑ そうですね。

Ⓐ *Tokidoki, tokai o hanarete nonbiri shitai desu ne.*

Ⓑ *Sō desu ne.*

Ⓐ I'd like to occasionally get away from the city to relax.

Ⓑ You're right.

2 ★ 川(かわ)で**のんびり**釣(つ)りでもしたいです。

★ *Kawa de nonbiri tsuri demo shitai desu.*

★ I'd like to relax and fish in a river.

50

ゆったり

Yuttari

Laid-back

ゆるやかで落ち着いていて、余裕がある様子。

For something to be leisurely easy and calm, providing for breathing room.

Point 時間について言う場合と、空間について言う場合がある。
Used both in situations regarding time and regarding space.

---

1 Ⓐ 旅行はどうでしたか。
Ⓑ きれいな景色を見ながら、**ゆったり**と過ごすことができました。

Ⓐ *Ryokō wa dō deshita ka?*
Ⓑ *Kirēna keshiki o minagara, yuttari to sugosu koto ga dekimashita.*

Ⓐ How was your trip?
Ⓑ I was able to see beautiful sights while spending time relaxing.

---

2 ★ ズボンは、**ゆったり**したデザインの方が好きです。

★ *Zubon wa, yuttari shita dezain no hō ga suki desu.*

★ I prefer pants with a laid-back design.

天気 Weather

51 52

どんより

Don'yori

Heavy

空が曇っていて、空気が重い天気の様子。

For the sky to be cloudy while the air is heavy.

どんよりする、どんよりV「曇る」、どんよりとV

Point 空全体を雲がおおって、重苦しい感じ。

For the entire sky to be covered in clouds, creating a gloomy feeling.

---

1 Ⓐ こんなにどんよりした天気だと、気持ちも暗くなるよ。

Ⓑ ほんとにそうだね。

Ⓐ *Konna ni don'yori shita tenki da to, kimochi mo kuraku naru yo.*

Ⓑ *Hontoni sō da ne.*

Ⓐ Being in this heavy weather even makes you feel darker.

Ⓑ That's really true.

---

2 Ⓐ 天気、どう？

Ⓑ どんより曇ってる。かさを持って行ったほうがいいかもしれない。

Ⓐ *Tenki, dō?*

Ⓑ *Don'yori kumotteru. Kasa o motte itta hō ga ī kamo shirenai.*

Ⓐ How's the weather?

Ⓑ There's heavy clouds. It might be better to bring an umbrella with you.

✲ 沈んだ気持ちを表す。 Used to indicate sullen emotions.

例 その日は、仕事でミスをして、気持ちがどんよりしていたんです。

Sono hi wa, shigoto de misu o shite, kimochi ga don'yori shite ita n desu.

I messed up at work that day, so my feelings were heavy.

52

ジメジメ

Damp; muggy

Jimejime

湿気(しっけ)が多(おお)く、不快(ふかい)な様子(ようす)。

For the weather to be humid and unpleasant.

Typical forms **ジメジメする、ジメジメとV**

Point 湿気(しっけ)が多(おお)く、風(かぜ)の通(とお)りが悪(わる)いこと。

For the humidity to be high, resulting in poor ventilation.

1

Ⓐ この部屋(へや)、**ジメジメ**してない？
Ⓑ そうだね。雨(あめ)が続(つづ)いてるからね。

Ⓐ *Kono heya, jimejime shitenai?*
Ⓑ *Sō da ne. Ame ga tsuzuiteru kara ne.*

Ⓐ Isn't this room muggy?
Ⓑ You're right. It's because it's been raining for a long time.

2

★ この辺(へん)は川(かわ)が近(ちか)いから、夏(なつ)になると**ジメジメ**するんだよ。

★ *Kono hen wa kawa ga chikai kara, natsu ni naru to jimejime suru n da yo.*

★ This area is near a river, so it gets damp in the summer.

Small Steps

✲ 陰気(いんき)で活気(かっき)のない様子(ようす)を表(あらわ)す。

Used to describe a state that is gloomy and unenergetic

例 **ジメジメ**した話(はなし)をして、ごめんなさい。もうやめます。

Jimejime shita hanashi o shite, gomennasai. Mō yamemasu.

I'm sorry for talking about something so gloomy. I'll stop.

人(ひと)の状態(じょうたい) A person's state

53

しーん
Shīn

Still

とても静(しず)かで、何(なん)の音(おと)もしない様子(ようす)。

For it to be very quiet, without a single sound.

Typical forms **しーんとV**「する」「なる」「静(しず)まる」

Point 非常(ひじょう)に静(しず)かなこと。急(きゅう)に静(しず)かになるときにもよく使(つか)う。
For things to be extremely quiet. Also often used when it suddenly becomes quiet.

---

1 Ⓐ 先生(せんせい)が「静(しず)かに！」って言(い)ったら、**しーん**となった。
Ⓑ 先生(せんせい)、怖(こわ)いからね。

Ⓐ *Sensē ga "Shizuka ni!" tte ittara, shīnto natta.*
Ⓑ *Sensē, kowai kara ne.*

Ⓐ When sensei said to "be quiet!", it become still.
Ⓑ Sensei is scary, after all.

---

2 ★ 話(はなし)を聞(き)いていた人(ひと)たちは皆(みな)、感動(かんどう)して、**しーん**となった。

★ *Hanashi o kīte ita hito tachi wa mina, kandō shite, shīnto natta.*

★ Everyone who heard the story was moved and became still.

54

ざわざわ

Zawazawa

Chattering

大勢集まった人たちの話し声がうるさく感じられる様子。

For a grouping of many people to be talking in what feels like a loud way.

ざわざわする、～とV「する」「なる」

Point 何かの会場で、集まった人がそれぞれにおしゃべりをしている様子など。

For situations such as events where gathered people are all talking among themselves.

---

1 Ⓐ 始まる時間になったのに、**ざわざわ**してるね。

Ⓑ 誰か注意したほうがいいかも。

Ⓐ *Hajimaru jikan ni natta noni, zawazawa shiteru ne.*

Ⓑ *Dareka chūi shita hō ga ī kamo.*

Ⓐ People are still chattering even though we've passed the starting time.

Ⓑ Maybe someone should warn them.

---

2 ★ 会場は人が多くて**ざわざわ**していた。

★ *Kaijō wa hito ga ōkute zawazawa shite ita.*

★ The venue had many people in it and was full of chatter.

心が落ち着かない様子を表す。

Used when one's heart/mind cannot calm down.

例 朝から胸が**ざわざわ**して落ち着かなかった。

Asa kara mune ga zawazawa shite ochitsuka nakatta.

My chest has been chattering from the morning and I couldn't calm down.

体調 Physical condition

55 54

カラカラ

Karakara

Parched

水分がなくなり、非常に乾いている状態。

To lose water content and become extremely dried out.

カラカラにV「なる」「乾く」、N「のど」がカラカラ、カラカラのN「天気」

Point のどが渇いて何か飲みたいときによく使う。

Often used when wanting to drink something because you feel thirsty.

---

1 Ⓐ しゃべりっぱなしで喉が**カラカラ**。
Ⓑ お疲れ様。お茶どうぞ。

Ⓐ *Shaberippanashi de nodo ga karakara.*
Ⓑ *Otsukaresama. Ocha dōzo.*

Ⓐ After talking so much, my throat is parched.
Ⓑ Good work. Have some tea.

---

2 Ⓐ スピーチ、がんばってね。
Ⓑ うん。緊張して、口の中が**カラカラ**。

Ⓐ *Supīchi, ganbatte ne.*
Ⓑ *Un. Kinchō shite, kuchi no naka ga karakara.*

Ⓐ You worked hard to give that speech.
Ⓑ Yes. I was nervous and now my mouth is parched.

Small Steps

✲「カラカラの～」は「とても乾いている～」という意味。

「カラカラの～」means "an extremely dry ～."

例 **カラカラの天気** *karakara no tenki*

Dry weather

56

Pekopeko

Starved

ペコペコ

ひどくお腹がすいた状態。
To become extremely hungry.

Typical forms ペコペコにV「なる」「お腹がすく」、N「お腹」がペコペコ

Point 短い言い方の「腹ペコ」もよく使う。
The shortened form,「腹ペコ」, is also used frequently.

---

1 Ⓐ もう1時過ぎてる。お腹**ペコペコ**。
Ⓑ ちょっと待って。今、用意するから。

Ⓐ *Mō ichiji sugiteru. Onaka pekopeko.*
Ⓑ *Chotto matte. Ima, yōi suru kara.*

Ⓐ It's already past 1. I'm starved.
Ⓑ Wait a second. I'll prepare something right now.

---

2 Ⓐ たくさん歩いたから、お腹が**ペコペコ**になった。
Ⓑ 私も。

Ⓐ *Takusan aruita kara, onaka ga pekopeko ni natta.*
Ⓑ *Watashi mo.*

Ⓐ I walked a lot, so now I'm starved.
Ⓑ Me too.

Small Steps

✲ ペコペコする：謝るときや人の機嫌をとるときなど、何度も頭を下げることを表す。
Used to express the action of bowing one's head multiple times when apologizing or trying to win someone's favor.

例 上司に**ペコペコする**のは好きじゃないんです。
Jōshi ni pekopeko suru nowa suki ja nai n desu.
I don't like having to kowtow to my boss.

57

55

シクシク

→p.22

Ache

Shikushiku

お腹や歯などに、それほど激しくないが痛みがずっと続く様子。

To have a long, continuous but not severe pain in one's stomach, tooth, and so on.

シクシクする、シクシクV「痛む」、シクシク Adj「痛い」

Point 痛みが、一定の強さで、止むことなく続くときに使う。
Used when feeling pain at a certain level that continues without stopping.

---

1 Ⓐ どうしました？
Ⓑ お昼を食べてから、お腹が**シクシク**するんです。

Ⓐ *Dō shimashita?*
Ⓑ *Ohiru o tabetekara, onaka ga shikushiku suru n desu.*

Ⓐ What's the matter?
Ⓑ After eating, my stomach has been aching.

---

2 ★ 歯が**シクシク**痛くて、何も食べられません。

★ *Ha ga shikushiku itakute, nani mo taberaremasen.*

★ My tooth has been aching and I can't eat anything.

58

ゴロゴロ

Gorogoro

Rumbling

お腹(なか)に異常(いじょう)にガスがたまったり、下痢(げり)したりしたときの状態(じょうたい)。

To have a large amount of gas in the stomach or to have diarrhea.

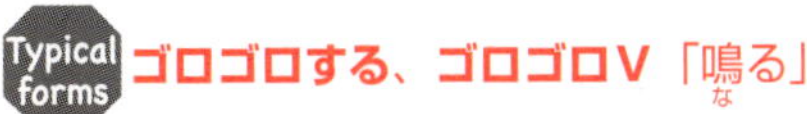
Typical forms ゴロゴロする、ゴロゴロV「鳴(な)る」

Point 実際(じっさい)にお腹(なか)の音(おと)がするときに使(つか)う。

Used when a stomach actually makes noise.

---

1 Ⓐ ゆうべ飲(の)み過(す)ぎたんじゃない？
Ⓑ うん、今朝(けさ)からお腹(なか)が**ゴロゴロ**してるよ。

Ⓐ *Yūbe nomi sugita n ja nai?*
Ⓑ *Un, kesa kara onaka ga gorogoro shiteru yo.*

Ⓐ Didn't you drink too much last night?
Ⓑ Yes, my stomach has been rumbling since this morning.

---

2 ★ お腹(なか)が**ゴロゴロ**鳴(な)るのをみんなに聞(き)かれて恥(は)ずかしい。

★ *Onaka ga gorogoro naru no o minna ni kikarete hazukashī.*

★ Everyone heard my stomach rumbling, so now I'm embarrassed.

59

56

ムカムカ →p.207

Queasy

Mukamuka

吐(は)き気(き)がして、気持(きも)ち悪(わる)いこと。

To feel like throwing up and sick.

Typical forms **ムカムカする、ムカムカ「胃(い)」が〜**

Point 不快(ふかい)なものが体(からだ)の中(なか)にとどまっていると感(かん)じるときに使(つか)う。

Used when feeling like something unpleasant is in one's body.

---

1 Ⓐ 最近(さいきん)、ときどき胃(い)が**ムカムカ**する。
Ⓑ えっ、赤(あか)ちゃんができたんじゃない？

Ⓐ *Saikin, tokidokī ga mukamuka suru.*
Ⓑ *Ett, akachan ga dekita n ja nai?*

Ⓐ Recently, my stomach has sometimes been feeling queasy.
Ⓑ What? Could you be pregnant?

---

2 Ⓐ どうしたの？　顔色(かおいろ)が悪(わる)いよ。
Ⓑ うん…。ちょっと**ムカムカ**して。

Ⓐ *Dō shita no? Kaoiro ga warui yo.*
Ⓑ *Un…. Chotto mukamuka shite.*

Ⓐ What's wrong? You look pale.
Ⓑ Yeah... I feel a little queasy.

60

チカチカ

Chikachika

Flickering

目(め)に強(つよ)い光(ひかり)が入(はい)って目(め)が痛(いた)い状態(じょうたい)。

For one's eyes to hurt because of looking at a strong light.

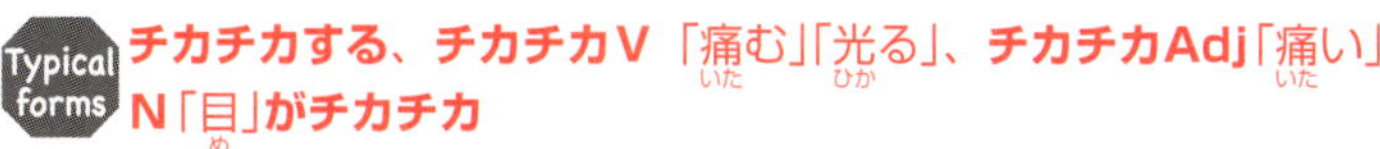

Typical forms **チカチカする、チカチカV**「痛(いた)む」「光(ひか)る」、**チカチカAdj**「痛(いた)い」、**N**「目(め)」**がチカチカ**

Point 光(ひかり)の刺激(しげき)によって、目(め)に痛(いた)みを感(かん)じるときに使(つか)う。

Used when feeling pain in one's eyes due to light stimulating them.

---

1 Ⓐ この部屋(へや)の電気(でんき)、まぶしくない？

Ⓑ そうだね。ちょっと目(め)が**チカチカ**するね。

Ⓐ *Kono heya no denki, mabushiku nai?*

Ⓑ *Sō da ne. Chotto me ga chikachika suru ne.*

Ⓐ Aren't the lights in this room bright?

Ⓑ Yes. My eyes are flickering a bit.

---

2 Ⓐ パソコンの使(つか)いすぎかなあ。目(め)が**チカチカ**する。

Ⓑ ときどき目(め)を休(やす)ませたほうがいいよ。

Ⓐ *Pasokon no tsukai sugi kanā. Me ga chikachika suru.*

Ⓑ *Tokidoki me o yasumaseta hō ga ī yo.*

Ⓐ I wonder if I'm using the computer too much. My eyes are flickering.

Ⓑ I think you should rest your eyes now and then.

61

57

ガンガン →p.73

Throbbing

Gangan

頭の中で大きな音が響くように、ひどく痛む様子。
To have one's head in extreme pain, as if a loud sound is inside of it.

ガンガンする、ガンガンV「痛む」、ガンガン Adj「痛い」、N「頭」がガンガン

Point 頭痛の痛みを表すときによく使う。
Often used to describe the pain of a headache.

---

1 Ⓐ どうしたの？ 何か、つらそうね。
Ⓑ 頭が**ガンガン**して…。

Ⓐ *Dō shita no? Nanka, tsurasō ne.*
Ⓑ *Atama ga gangan shite….*

Ⓐ What's the matter? It seems like you're having a tough time.
Ⓑ My head is throbbing...

---

2 Ⓐ 昨日の帰りは大変だったそうですね。
Ⓑ ええ。雨にぬれるし、頭は**ガンガン**痛くなるし。

Ⓐ *Kinō no kaeri wa taihen datta sō desu ne.*
Ⓑ *Ē. Ame ni nureru shi, atama wa gangan itaku naru shi.*

Ⓐ It seems like you had a tough time getting home last night.
Ⓑ Yes. I got wet from the rain, and my head throbbed and hurt.

62

クラクラ

Kurakura

めまいがして倒れそうな状態。

To be dizzy and nearly falling over.

クラクラする、N「頭」「目」がクラクラ

Point めまいがしたとき、また、難しい問題が起きたときによく使う。

Often used when feeling dizzy, or when a difficult problem arises.

---

1 Ⓐ さっき、いすから立つ時にちょっと**クラクラ**した。

Ⓑ 大丈夫？　ご飯、ちゃんと食べてる？

Ⓐ *Sakki isu kara tatsu toki ni chotto kurakura shita.*

Ⓑ *Daijōbu? Gohan, chanto tabeteru?*

Ⓐ I felt a little dizzy just now when I stood up from my chair.

Ⓑ Are you okay? Are you eating properly?

---

2 ★ あー、頭が**クラクラ**する。熱があるかも。

★ *Ā, atama ga kurakura suru. Netsu ga aru kamo.*

★ Oh, my head feels dizzy. I might have a fever.

✲ 比ゆ的な表現もある。

This can also be used as a metaphorical expression.

例 費用が 50 万円かかると聞いて、**クラクラ**してきた。

Hiyō ga gojū man en kakaru to kīte, kurakura shite kita.

When I heard it would cost 500,000 yen, I felt dizzy.

63

58

ゾクゾク

Zokuzoku

Chilly

風邪などで寒さを感じる様子。

To feel cold (temperature) due to a cold (sickness).

ゾクゾクする、ゾクゾク Adj「寒い」、N「背中」「背筋」がゾクゾク

Point 風邪で熱があるときに感じる寒さ。

The coldness felt when having a fever because of a cold.

1

Ⓐ 熱はないんですが、**ゾクゾク**して寒いんです。
Ⓑ じゃ、風邪のひき始めかもしれませんよ。

Ⓐ *Netsu wa nai n desu ga, zokuzoku shite samui n desu.*
Ⓑ *Ja, kaze no hiki hajime kamo shiremasen yo.*

Ⓐ I don't have a fever, but I feel chilly and cold.
Ⓑ In that case, you might have started to get a cold.

2

★ 背中が**ゾクゾク**してきたので、今日は早く寝ます。

★ *Senaka ga zokuzoku shite kita node, kyō wa hayaku nemasu.*

★ My back is feeling chilly, so I'm going to go to bed early today.

✲ 恐怖や興奮を表す表現もある。

Also used as an expression of fear and excitement.

例 決勝がどんな試合になるか、今から**ゾクゾク**する。

Kesshō ga donna shiai ni naru ka, ima kara zokuzoku suru.

I feel chills thinking about what kind of match the finals will be.

64

ブルブル

Buruburu

Shivering

寒(さむ)くて体(からだ)がふるえる状態(じょうたい)。

For one's body to be shivering due to the cold.

Typical forms ブルブルV「する」「ふるえる」、N「体(からだ)」がブルブル

Point 特(とく)に体(からだ)が震(ふる)えるときに使(つか)う。

Used when one's body shakes notably.

---

1 Ⓐ 大丈夫(だいじょうぶ)？ ブルブルふるえてるじゃない。
Ⓑ うん…寒(さむ)い。

Ⓐ *Daijōbu? Buruburu furueteru ja nai.*
Ⓑ *Un…samui.*

Ⓐ Are you okay? You're shivering.
Ⓑ Yeah... I'm cold.

---

2 ★ 雪(ゆき)の中(なか)でブルブルふるえて立(た)っていました。

★ *Yuki no naka de buruburu furuete tatte imashita.*

★ He was shaking standing in the snow.

65

59

へとへと

Hetoheto

Exhausted

ひどく疲(つか)れて、何(なに)もできない状態(じょうたい)。

To be extremely tired and unable to do anything.

へとへとだ、へとへとにV「疲(つか)れる」

Point エネルギーが切(き)れたような状態(じょうたい)。

The state of feeling as though one is out of energy.

---

1 Ⓐ あー、もう、**へとへと**。これ以上(いじょう)できないよ。

Ⓑ そうだね。もうこれで終(お)わりにしよう。

Ⓐ *Ā, mō, hetoheto. Kore ijō deki nai yo.*

Ⓑ *Sō dane. Mō kore de owari ni shiyō.*

Ⓐ Oh, I'm just exhausted. I can't do any more.

Ⓑ Yeah. Let's end it with this.

---

2 ★ 今日(きょう)は朝(あさ)から夜(よる)までずっと忙(いそが)しくて、**へとへと**に疲(つか)れた。

★ *Kyō wa asa kara yoru made zutto isogashikute, hetoheto ni tsukareta.*

★ I've been busy today from morning to night, and now I'm exhausted.

66

ぐったり

Guttari

Worn out

疲(つか)れや熱(ねつ)のために力(ちから)が抜(ぬ)けたような状態(じょうたい)。

To have no strength due to fatigue or heat.

ぐったりする、ぐったりだ、ぐったりとV 「疲(つか)れる」「倒(たお)れる」

Point 疲(つか)れや熱(ねつ)などで力(ちから)を失(うしな)って元気(げんき)が出(で)ない状態(じょうたい)。

The state of losing one's strength and being unable to be energetic because of fatigue, fever, and so on.

---

1 Ⓐ 疲(つか)れたー！　もう**ぐったり**。

Ⓑ お疲(つか)れ様(さま)！　今日(きょう)はよく寝(ね)て。

Ⓐ *Tsukaretā! Mō guttari.*

Ⓑ *Otsukaresama! Kyō wa yoku nete.*

Ⓐ I'm so tired! I'm worn out.

Ⓑ Good work! You should get a good night's sleep tonight.

---

2 Ⓐ お子(こ)さんの具合(ぐあい)は？

Ⓑ 熱(ねつ)がかなりあって、**ぐったり**しています。

Ⓐ *Okosan no guai wa?*

Ⓑ *Netsu ga kanari atte, guttari shite imasu.*

Ⓐ How is your child doing?

Ⓑ She has a pretty bad fever, so she's worn out.

全部(ぜんぶ)クリア　Everything cleared

67　60

はっきり

Hakkiri

Clearly

形(かたち)などが、どんなものか、わかりやすい様子(ようす)。

For the shape, etc. of something to be easily understood.

はっきりする、はっきりV「言(い)う」、はっきりとV

Point 曖昧(あいまい)なところがなく、それがどんなものか、よくわかる。

For the nature of something to be clear and not vague at all.

1
Ⓐ それが、その・・・あの・・・
Ⓑ 何(なに)？　**はっきり**言(い)ってください。

Ⓐ *Sorega, sono…ano…*
Ⓑ *Nani? Hakkiri itte kudasai.*

Ⓐ That's, ah... um...
Ⓑ What? Say it clearly, please.

2
★ もう少(すこ)し**はっきり**書(か)いてください。

★ *Mō sukoshi hakkiri kaite kudasai.*

★ Could you please write it a little more clearly?

68

くっきり

Kukkiri

Distinctly

姿や形が非常にはっきりしている様子。

For the figure or shape of something to be extremely clear.

Typical forms 
くっきりする、くっきりV「写る」「見える」「浮かぶ」、くっきりとV、くっきりしたN

Point 線が太かったり、色が濃かったりして、見て、その部分がよくわかるときに使う。

Used when something is clearly recognizable due to thick lines or dark color.

1

Ⓐ 日焼けのあとが**くっきり**残ってる。
Ⓑ 昨日、ずっと外にいたからね。

Ⓐ *Hiyake no ato ga kukkiri nokotteru.*
Ⓑ *Kinō, zutto soto ni ita kara ne.*

Ⓐ The signs of where you were sunburned have been distinctly left behind.
Ⓑ It's because I was outside all of yesterday.

2

★ 今日は富士山が**くっきり**見えるね。

★ *Kyō wa Fujisan ga kukkiri mieru ne.*

★ Mt. Fuji is distinctly visible today, isn't it?

69

61

すっきり →p. 203

Sukkiri

Refreshed

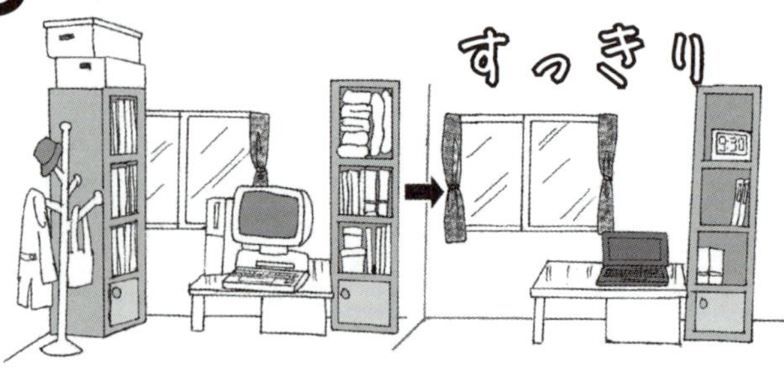

余計なものや曖昧なところがなく、気持ちよく感じられる様子。

For something to feel good, with no extraneous or ambiguous elements.

Typical forms すっきりする、すっきりV「片付く」、すっきりとV

Point 余計なものを取ったあとの気持ちよさを表す。

Expresses the pleasant feeling of getting rid of something unnecessary.

---

1 Ⓐ この部屋、**すっきり**したね。
Ⓑ そうでしょ？　家具を減らしたから。

Ⓐ *Kono heya, sukkiri shita ne.*
Ⓑ *Sō desho? Kagu o herashita kara.*

Ⓐ This room really has been refreshed.
Ⓑ Hasn't it? It's because I got rid of some furniture.

---

2 ★ 髪、切ったんだ。ずいぶん、**すっきり**したね。

★ *Kami, kitta n da. Zuibun, sukkiri shita ne.*

★ You cut your hair. You look quite refreshed.

70

さっぱり

→p.129、p.202

Cleanly

Sappari

全然～ない。

Not ~ at all.

さっぱりする、さっぱりVない「わからない」、**さっぱりとV**

Point 「わかる」「売れる」「見る」「聞く」などの動詞につく。

Attached to verbs such as understand, sell, see, and hear.

---

1 Ⓐ どう？　少しは売れた？

Ⓑ いや。こんな天気じゃ、だめ。**さっぱり**売れないよ。

Ⓐ *Dō? Sukoshi wa ureta?*

Ⓑ *Iya. Konna tenki ja, dame. Sappari urenai yo.*

Ⓐ So? Sell any?

Ⓑ No. It's no good in this weather. It won't sell at all.

---

2 ★ パソコンのことなんて、私には**さっぱり**わからない。

★ *Pasokon no koto nante, watashi ni wa sappari wakaranai.*

★ I don't understand a thing about computers.

71

62

すっかり

Sukkari

Completely

完全に、何から何まで。

Entirely, from start to finish.

すっかりV「変わる」「片付く」「なくす」、**～とV**

Point 残るところがなく全部であること。

Everything, without exception.

---

1 Ⓐ 最近、引っ越したんでしょ。もう、落ち着いた？
Ⓑ はい、おかげさまで。**すっかり**片付きました。

Ⓐ *Saikin, hikkoshita n de sho. Mō, ochitsuita?*
Ⓑ *Hai, okagesama de. Sukkari katazukimashita.*

Ⓐ You moved recently, right? Have things calmed down?
Ⓑ Yes, thanks to you. Things have been completely cleaned up.

---

2 ★ 彼は会社に勤めるようになって、**すっかり**変わった。

★ *Kare wa kaisha ni tsutomeru yō ni natte, sukkari kawatta.*

★ He changed completely after he started to work for a company.

72

バッチリ

Perfectly

Bacchiri

順調に、準備が十分、完璧。
じゅんちょう　じゅんび　じゅうぶん　かんぺき

Favorably, with adequate preparations, flawlessly.

バッチリだ、Nはバッチリ

Point 準備が完璧なときによく使う。
じゅんび　かんぺき　つか

Often used when preparations for something are perfect.

---

1 Ⓐ 田中さん、プレゼンの準備は大丈夫？
た なか　じゅんび　だいじょうぶ

Ⓑ うん、今回は**バッチリ**。
こんかい

Ⓐ *Tanaka san, purezen no junbi wa daijōbu?*

Ⓑ *Un, konkai wa bacchiri.*

Ⓐ Tanaka-san, are your presentation preparations going okay?

Ⓑ Yes, this one is going perfectly.

---

2 ★ 料理もあるし、ワインもあるし、**バッチリ**だね。
りょうり

★ *Ryōri mo aru shi, wain mo aru shi, bacchiri da ne.*

★ They have food, they have wine, they're perfect.

程度(ていど) Degree

73 63

めちゃくちゃ／めっちゃ →p.103

Super

非常(ひじょう)に、すごく。

Extremely, a lot.

Typical forms めちゃくちゃ Adj「面白(おもしろ)い」「楽(たの)しい」

Point 程度(ていど)が非常(ひじょう)に強(つよ)いことを表(あらわ)す。会話(かいわ)では「めっちゃ」もよく使(つか)われる。
Expresses that the degree of something is extremely strong. めっちゃ is often used in spoken Japanese, too.

1
Ⓐ ケーキ、どう？
Ⓑ **めちゃくちゃ**おいしい。

Ⓐ *Kēki, dō?*
Ⓑ *Mechakucha oishī.*

Ⓐ How is the cake?
Ⓑ It's super delicious.

2
★ 見(み)て、見(み)て、パンダの赤(あか)ちゃん。**めっちゃ**かわいい！

★ *Mite, mite, panda no akachan. Meccha kawaī!*

★ Look, look, a baby panda! It's super cute!

うんと

Unto

Lots

たくさん、非常に。

Lots, extremely.

Typical forms うんと V「食べる」「飲む」「勉強する」、うんと Adj「楽しい」「高い」

Point 量が多いことを漠然と言う。

Vaguely states that the amount of something is large.

---

1 Ⓐ〈小さい子どもに〉**うんと**食べて、大きくなってね。

Ⓑ はい。

Ⓐ *Unto tabete, ōkiku natte ne.*

Ⓑ *Hai.*

Ⓐ (To a small child) Eat lots and get big, okay?

Ⓑ Okay.

---

2 ★ 医者になりたいんですか。じゃ、**うんと**勉強しないと。

★ *Isha ni naritai n desu ka? Ja, unto benkyō shinai to.*

★ So you want to become a doctor? In that case, you need to study a lot.

その他　Other

75　64

そっくり

Sokkuri

Exactly

非常によく似ていること。

To be extremely similar.

Nと(に)そっくりだ

Point 見た目だけでなく、内容についても言う。

Used about content, not only appearance.

1
Ⓐ たけしさんって、お父さんと**そっくり**ですね。
Ⓑ よくそう言われます。

Ⓐ *Takeshi san tte, otōsan to sokkuri desu ne.*
Ⓑ *Yoku sō iwaremasu.*

Ⓐ Takeshi-san, you look exactly like your father.
Ⓑ I get told that a lot.

2
★ この映画のストーリー、前に見たマンガと**そっくり**。

★ *Kono ēga no sutōrī, mae ni mita manga to sokkuri.*

★ The story of that movie is the exact same as a manga I've read before.

76

そろそろ

Sorosoro

Just about

まもなく。

Shortly.

Typical forms そろそろV「出かける」

Point「もう、その時間だ」と言いたいときに使う。

Used when one wants to say It's that time already.

---

1 Ⓐ もう2時だ。**そろそろ**出かけましょう。
Ⓑ そうですね。

Ⓐ *Mō ni ji da. Sorosoro dekakemashō.*
Ⓑ *Sō desu ne.*

Ⓐ It's already 2. We should just about go.
Ⓑ You're right.

---

2 ★ ねえ、見ないの？ **そろそろ**試合、始まるよ。

★ *Nē, minai no? Sorosoro shiai, hajimaru yo.*

★ Hey, you're not going to watch? The match is about to start shortly.

77

でこぼこ(凸凹)

Bumpy

Dekoboko

平ら(たい)でなく、出(で)ているところとへこんでいるところがある様子(ようす)。

To not be flat, but instead to have places that stick out and curve inward.

Typical forms **でこぼこV**「です」、**でこぼこN**「道(みち)」

Point 漢字(かんじ)は「凸凹(でこぼこ)」。(「でこ」+「ぼこ」でなく)二字(にじ)で「でこぼこ」と読(よ)む。

Written in kanji as「凸凹」. (Not「でこ」+「ぼこ」) The two kanji are read「でこぼこ」.

---

1 Ⓐ この道(みち)、**でこぼこ**してて、歩(ある)きにくいね。
Ⓑ うん。

Ⓐ *Kono michi, dekoboko shitete, aruki nikui ne.*
Ⓑ *Un.*

Ⓐ This road is bumpy and hard to walk on.
Ⓑ Yes.

---

2 ★ 表面(ひょうめん)はツルツルしているかと思(おも)ったら、意外(いがい)と**でこぼこ**していた。

★ *Hyōmen wa tsurutsuru shite iru ka tōmottara, igai to dekoboko shite ita.*

★ While I thought the surface was smooth, it was surprisingly bumpy.

PART 4

心(こころ)の状態(じょうたい)を表(あらわ)す

Indicating a mental/emotional state

楽(たの)しい
Happy

緊張(きんちょう)・不安(ふあん)
Nervous / Anxious

感動(かんどう)
Powerful emotion

失望(しつぼう)
Disillusionment

不確(ふたし)か
Uncertainty

驚(おどろ)き
Surprise

我慢(がまん)の限界(げんかい)
The limit of one's patience

混乱(こんらん)
Confusion

後悔(こうかい)・不満(ふまん)
Regret / Dissatisfaction

心(こころ)の変化(へんか)
An emotional change

気分(きぶん)
Feeling

怒(いか)り
Anger

楽しい Happy

1

65

ワクワク

Excited

Wakuwaku

予定されている楽しいことなどを思い、期待で胸がふくらむ様子。
To be excited and waiting in anticipation for something enjoyable that is supposed to come.

ワクワクする、ワクワクとV、N「胸」「心」がワクワク

Point 楽しみにしているイベントの前によく使う。
Often used before an event one is looking forward to.

1 Ⓐ 4月から社会人だね。
Ⓑ はい。少し不安もありますが、**ワクワク**しています。

Ⓐ *Si-gatsu kara shakai jin da ne.*
Ⓑ *Hai. Sukoshi fuan mo arimasu ga, wakuwaku shite imasu.*

Ⓐ So you're going to be working starting in April.
Ⓑ Yes. I'm a little anxious, but I'm excited.

2 ★ 初めてパリに行くので、**ワクワク**しています。

★ *Hajimete pari ni iku node, wakuwaku shite imasu.*

★ This will be my first time going to Paris, and I'm excited.

2

ウキウキ

Ukiuki

Lighthearted

心が明るく弾んでいる様子。

To be excited with a cheerful mind.

ウキウキする、ウキウキとV、N「胸」「心」がウキウキ

Point 楽しさやうれしさから落ち着かないときに使う。

Used when unable to calm down because of excitement or joy.

---

1 Ⓐ 桜が咲き始めると、なんだか**ウキウキ**してくる。

Ⓑ 春が来た、って感じがするよね。

Ⓐ *Sakura ga saki hajimeru to, nandaka ukiuki shite kuru.*

Ⓑ *Haru ga kita, tte kanji ga suru yo ne.*

Ⓐ For some reason, I start to feel lighthearted when the cherry blossoms begin to bloom.

Ⓑ It feels like spring has come.

---

2 ★ 今日、デートがあるから、姉が**ウキウキ**していました。

★ *Kyō, dēto ga aru kara ane ga ukiuki shite imashita.*

★ My big sister was lighthearted because she has a date today.

3

66

そわそわ

Sowasowa

Restless

予定(よてい)されていることが気(き)になって、落(お)ち着(つ)かない様子(ようす)。

To be unsettled because one is worried about something that is scheduled to come.

そわそわする、そわそわとV

Point 心(こころ)が落(お)ち着(つ)かず、じっとしていられない様子(ようす)の人(ひと)について言(い)う。

Used to describe someone who cannot stay still because their emotional state will not calm down.

---

1 Ⓐ 彼(かれ)、何(なん)か朝(あさ)から**そわそわ**してない？
Ⓑ 今日(きょう)、デートみたいだよ。

Ⓐ *Kare, nan ka asa kara sowasowa shite nai?*
Ⓑ *Kyō, dēto mitai da yo.*

Ⓐ Hasn't he been acting restless since this morning?
Ⓑ It sounds like he has a date today.

---

2 Ⓐ 〈病院(びょういん)で〉ひろしさん、**そわそわ**してるね。
Ⓑ それはそうでしょう。もうすぐ父親(ちちおや)になるんだから。

Ⓐ *[Byōin de] Hiroshi san, sowasowa shiteru ne.*
Ⓑ *Sore wa sō deshō. Mōsugu chichioya ni naru n dakara.*

Ⓐ (At a hospital) Hiroshi-san is acting restless.
Ⓑ Of course he is. He's going to be a father soon.

4

ルンルン

Runrun

Euphoric

良いことが起きるのを興奮して待つときの心がおどる様子。

To be excited as one waits for something good to happen.

ルンルンする、ルンルンとV、ルンルンN「気分」

Point 楽しいことやうれしいことがあり、心がおどるような気分。

To feel one's heart dancing because of something exciting or joyful occurring.

---

1 Ⓐ 彼女、明日からハワイに旅行に行くそうですよ。

Ⓑ じゃ、**ルンルン**気分だね。

Ⓐ *Kanojo, ashita kara hawai ni ryokō ni iku sō desu yo.*

Ⓑ *Ja, runrun kibun da ne.*

Ⓐ It sounds like she's going to go on a trip to Hawaii from tomorrow.

Ⓑ She must be euphoric, then.

---

2 Ⓐ 宝くじが当たったんだって？

Ⓑ うん、5万円。だから、ちょっと**ルンルン**してる。

Ⓐ *Takara kuji ga atatta n datte?*

Ⓑ *Un, go-man-en. Dakara, chotto runrun shiteru.*

Ⓐ So you won the lottery?

Ⓑ Yes, 50,000 yen. That's why I'm a little euphoric.

緊張・不安 Nervous / Anxious

5 67

ドキドキ

Heart-pounding

Dokidoki

不安や喜びで心臓の動きが速くなる状態。

To have one's heart beating faster because of anxiety or joy.

Typical forms ドキドキする、ドキドキとV、N「胸」「心」がドキドキ

Point 心臓が動く音を表した言葉。

A term used to express the sound of one's heart beating.

---

1 Ⓐ ああ、もうすぐ電話来る。どうしよう、ドキドキする。

Ⓑ 大丈夫、落ち着いて。

Ⓐ *Ā, mōsugu denwa kuru. Dōshiyō, dokidoki suru.*

Ⓑ *Daijōbu, ochitsuite.*

Ⓐ Oh, they're about to call. What should I do, my heart is pounding.

Ⓑ It's fine, just calm down.

---

2 ★ 面接の前はいつもドキドキしちゃう。

★ *Mensetsu no mae wa itsumo dokidoki shichau.*

★ My heart always pounds before an interview.

6

ハラハラ

Harahara

Uneasy

危険な状況を前に、大変なことが起きないか、心配する様子。

To be worried that something bad is going to happen before a dangerous situation occurs.

ハラハラする、ハラハラとV

Point 自分以外の何かが危険にあるときに使う。

Used when something other than one's self is in danger.

---

1 Ⓐ もう、**ハラハラ**したよ。落ちたら、大けがしてたよ。

Ⓑ 大丈夫だよ。ちゃんと注意してるから。

Ⓐ *Mō, harahara shita yo. Ochitara, ōkega shiteta yo.*

Ⓑ *Daijōbu da yo. Chanto chūi shiteru kara.*

Ⓐ I was feeling uneasy. You would have been majorly injured if you fell.

Ⓑ It's fine. I was properly careful, you know.

---

2 ★ 昨日の試合は、勝つか負けるか、最後まで**ハラハラ**させられた。

★ *Kinō no shiai wa, katsu ka makeru ka, saigo made harahara saserareta.*

★ I was feeling uneasy about yesterday's match until the very end, not knowing if the team was going to win or lose.

7

ヒヤヒヤ

Hiyahiya

Nervous

危険を感じたことが現実にならないかと、不安や恐怖を感じる様子。

To feel anxiety or fear about something dangerous possibly becoming a reality.

Typical forms **ヒヤヒヤする、ヒヤヒヤとV**

Point 自分自身が危険にあるときに使う。

Used when one's self is in danger.

---

1 Ⓐ 間に合って良かったね。
Ⓑ 遅れるんじゃないかと、**ヒヤヒヤ**したよ。

Ⓐ *Ma ni ate yokatta ne.*
Ⓑ *Okureru n ja nai ka to, hiyahiya shita yo.*

Ⓐ It's good that you made it in time.
Ⓑ I was nervous that I would be late.

---

2 ★ 嘘がバレたらどうしようと**ヒヤヒヤ**した。

★ *Uso ga baretara dōshiyō to hiyahiya shita.*

★ I was nervous thinking about what I would do if my lie got found out.

Small Steps

✻ 瞬間的に危険を感じたとき、「ヒヤッとする」を使う。

「ヒヤッとする」is used when a momentary danger is felt.

8

68

ビクビク

Timid

Bikubiku

常に不安や恐怖を感じながら、気持ちが小さくなる様子。

To psychologically shrink because of a constant feeling of anxiety or fear.

Typical forms **ビクビクする、ビクビクとV**

Point 恐怖にふるえているような心の状態。
The state of a heart trembling in fear.

---

1 Ⓐ そんなに**ビクビク**しないで。
Ⓑ すみません。初めての経験なので、緊張して。

Ⓐ *Sonna ni bikubiku shinaide.*
Ⓑ *Sumimasen. Hajimete no kēken nanode, kinchō shite.*

Ⓐ Don't be so timid.
Ⓑ I'm sorry. This is my first time, so I'm nervous.

---

2 Ⓐ 店長、すぐ怒るよね。
Ⓑ うん…。みんな、**ビクビク**してるよ。

Ⓐ *Tenchō, sugu okoru yo ne.*
Ⓑ *Un…. Minna, bikubiku shiteru yo.*

Ⓐ The manager gets angry so quickly.
Ⓑ Yes... Everyone's feeling timid.

9

おどおど

Apprehensive

Odoodo

緊張や恐れが強く、自信が全く持てず、落ち着かない様子。

To feel strongly nervous or fearful, resulting in having no sense of confidence or stability.

Typical forms **おどおどする、おどおどとV**

Point 「ビクビク」に比べ、落ち着きのなさが目立つ特徴。

Compared to「ビクビク」, this term is used when one's lack of calmness is noticeable.

---

1 Ⓐ 何も悪いことしてないんだから、**おどおど**することないよ。

Ⓑ そうだね。

Ⓐ *Nani mo warui koto shitenai n dakara, odoodo suru koto nai yo.*

Ⓑ *Sō da ne.*

Ⓐ You haven't done anything wrong, so don't feel so apprehensive.

Ⓑ You're right.

---

2 ★ 社長はすぐ怒るから、みんな、社長の前では**おどおど**しちゃうんだよね。

★ *Shachō wa sugu okoru kara, minna, shachō no mae de wa odoodo shichau n da yo ne.*

★ The President is so fast to get mad that everyone is apprehensive in front of him.

感動(かんどう) Powerful emotion

10

グッと

Gutto

Gripped

何(なに)かを見(み)たり聞(き)いたりしたときに、感動(かんどう)して心(こころ)を奪(うば)われる様子(ようす)。

To be emotionally moved and captivated when seeing or hearing something.

グッとV「来(く)る」

Point 感動(かんどう)や強(つよ)い感情(かんじょう)が急(きゅう)に胸(むね)にわき上(あ)がること。

For one's heart to well up suddenly due to being moved or because of strong emotions.

1
Ⓐ 今日(きょう)、面接(めんせつ)した人(ひと)はどうですか。
Ⓑ うーん、悪(わる)くないんだけど、もう一(ひと)つ**グッと**来(く)るものがなかったな。

Ⓐ *Kyō, mensetsu sita hito wa dō desu ka?*
Ⓑ *Ūn, waruku nai n dakedo, mō hitotsu gutto kuru mono ga nakatta na.*

Ⓐ How was the person you interviewed today?
Ⓑ Hmm, not bad, but he was missing one thing that gripped me.

2
Ⓐ 彼女(かのじょ)のスピーチ、よかったね。
Ⓑ うん、**グッと**来(き)た。

Ⓐ *Kanojo no supīchi, yokatta ne.*
Ⓑ *Un, gutto kita.*

Ⓐ Wasn't her speech good?
Ⓑ Yes, it gripped me.

11

キュンと

Moved

Kyunto

感動して、瞬間的に胸が締めつけられるような思いになること。

To be emotionally moved, causing one to momentarily feel like their chest is tight.

Typical forms **キュンとする、キュンとなる、N「胸」「心」がキュンと**

Point 恋愛に関する表現として使われることが多い。
Often used as an expression related to love.

---

1 Ⓐ あんな小さな子があんなことを言うなんて！
Ⓑ 胸が**キュンと**なるよね。

Ⓐ *Anna chīsana ko ga anna koto o iu nante!*
Ⓑ *Mune ga kyunto naru yo ne.*

Ⓐ I can't believe such a small child would say something like that!
Ⓑ It was moving, wasn't it?

---

2 ★ たった一言だけど、メールもらった時は胸が**キュンと**したよ。

★ *Tatta hitokoto dakedo, mēru moratta toki wa mune ga kyunto shita yo.*

★ It was just a word, but my heart was moved when I got the email.

12

70

じーんと

Touching

Jīnto

感動が心の中に広がっていく様子。
To feel a sense of being moved spreading throughout one's heart.

じーんとする、じーんとV「来る」

Point 「心に響く」「胸が熱くなる」ような感覚を表す。
Expresses something reverberating in the heart or for one's chest to grow hot.

---

1 Ⓐ その映画、そんなにいいの？
Ⓑ それはもう。何度見ても**じーんと**来るんだ。

Ⓐ *Sono ēga, sonna ni ī no?*
Ⓑ *Sore wa mō. Nando mitemo jīnto kuru n da.*

Ⓐ Is that movie that good?
Ⓑ Of course. It's touching no matter how many times I see it.

---

2 ★ その話は私も知ってる。**じーんと**来るよね。

★ *Sono hanashi wa watashi mo shitteru. Jīnto kuru yo ne.*

★ I know that story, too. It's touching, isn't it?

13

しみじみ

Shimijimi

Keenly

心の底から深く感じる様子。
To be deeply moved from the bottom of one's heart.

しみじみする、しみじみとV、N「人生」しみじみ

Point 感情が心に深くしみ込んでいる感じ。
The feeling of emotions penetrating deep into one's heart.

1

Ⓐ 大変だったね。
Ⓑ うん。自分でもよくやったと、**しみじみ**思うよ。

Ⓐ *Taihen datta ne.*
Ⓑ *Un. Jibun demo yoku yatta to, shimijimi omou yo.*

Ⓐ That must have been tough.
Ⓑ Yes, even I keenly think that I did a good job.

2

★ 子どもの頃は楽しかったなあと、**しみじみ**思います。

★ *Kodomo no koro wa tanoshikatta nā to, shimijimi omoimasu.*

★ I keenly feel that I had fun when I was a child.

14

ウルウル

Uruuru

Teary-eyed

感動して涙が出るような気持ち。

To be moved to the point of tears.

Typical forms **ウルウルする、ウルウルとV、N「目」がウルウル**

Point 感動して涙が出て、あふれそうなときに使う。

To be moved to tears, to the point that they may overflow.

---

1 Ⓐ すごく感動してたね。
Ⓑ うん…。ちょっと**ウルウル**しちゃった。

Ⓐ *Sugoku kandō shiteta ne.*
Ⓑ *Un…. Chotto uruuru shichatta.*

Ⓐ That was so moving.
Ⓑ Yes... I got a little teary-eyed.

---

2 ★ これ、子ども向けのアニメだけど、大人でも**ウルウル**しますよ。

★ *Kore, kodomo muke no anime dakedo, otona demo uruuru shimasu yo.*

★ This is a cartoon for children, but even adults will get teary-eyed watching it.

先望(しつぼう) Disillusionment

15 71

がっかり

Gakkari

Disappointed

思(おも)い通(どお)りに行(い)かず、失望(しつぼう)して力(ちから)が抜(ぬ)ける様子(ようす)。

For things to not go as expected, to be disappointed and dispirited.

がっかりする、がっかりとV

Point 期待(きたい)に反(はん)する結果(けっか)が起(お)きたときに使(つか)う。

Used when something occurs that is contrary to one's expectations.

1
Ⓐ 無料(むりょう)コンサート、中止(ちゅうし)になったって。
Ⓑ うそー。**がっかり**。

Ⓐ *Muryō konsāto, chūshi ni natta tte.*
Ⓑ *Usō. Gakkari.*

Ⓐ I heard the free concert was canceled.
Ⓑ No way! What a disappointment.

2
★ いい人(ひと)だと思(おも)っていたので、それを聞(き)いて、**がっかり**しました。

★ *Ī hito da to omotte ita node, sore o kīte, gakkari shimashita.*

★ I thought he was a good person, so when I heard that, I was disappointed.

16

がっくり

Gakkuri

Let down

残念なことが起きて、急に元気をなくす様子。

To suddenly lose one's energy after something unfortunate happens.

Typical forms がっくりする、がっくりV「来る」、がっくりとV

Point 力が抜けてしまう点が最大の特徴。

Most notable for the fact that the term involves the feeling of strength leaving one's body.

---

1 Ⓐ お父さん、検査結果聞いてどうでした？
Ⓑ はい、健康には自信あったので、**がっくり**していました。

Ⓐ *Otōsan, kensa kekka kīte dō deshita?*
Ⓑ *Hai, kenkō ni wa jishin atta node, gakkuri shite imashita.*

Ⓐ What happened after dad heard his test results?
Ⓑ Well, he was pretty confident about his health, so he felt let down.

---

2 Ⓐ 彼、代表に選ばれなかったんだ。
Ⓑ そう。知らせを聞いて、**がっくり**してたよ。

Ⓐ *Kare, daihyō ni erabare nakatta n da.*
Ⓑ *Sō. Shirase o kīte, gakkuri shiteta yo.*

Ⓐ So he wasn't chosen to be the representative?
Ⓑ Well, he was pretty confident about his health, so he felt let down.

17

しょんぼり

Dejected

Shonbori

元気(げんき)がなく、さびしそうな様子(ようす)。

To have no energy, to seem sad.

しょんぼりする、しょんぼりとV

Point 話(はな)し相手(あいて)がいない場合(ばあい)もあれば、話(はなし)をする気分(きぶん)でない場合(ばあい)もある。

Can be used both for situations where there is no one to talk to, as well as situations where one does not feel like talking.

1

Ⓐ どうしたの？　そんなに**しょんぼり**して。

Ⓑ お客(きゃく)さんを怒(おこ)らせてしまったんです。

Ⓐ *Dō shita no? Sonna ni shonbori shite.*

Ⓑ *Okyakusan o okorasete shimatta n desu.*

Ⓐ What's the matter? You seem so dejected.

Ⓑ A customer got mad at me.

2

★ 田中(たなか)さん、何(なに)かあったの？　一人(ひとり)で**しょんぼり**してたけど。

★ *Tanaka san, nani kātta no? Hitori de shonbori shiteta kedo.*

★ Did something happen to Tanaka-san? She was all alone and seemed dejected.

不確か Uncertainty

18

ぼうっと

Bōtto

Blankly

72

何にも焦点が合わずに意識がぼやけている状態、ぼやけて見える状態。

To have no focus and to have a blurry consciousness, or to see things in a blurry way.

Typical forms ぼうっとする、ぼうっとV「考える」

Point「何も見ていない、何も考えていない」ような状態。

A state where one is not looking or thinking about anything.

---

1 Ⓐ 違うところにファックスを送ったんですか。

Ⓑ すみません、**ぼうっと**していました。

Ⓐ *Chigau tokoro ni fakkusu o okutta n desu ka?*

Ⓑ *Sumimasen, bōtto shite imashita.*

Ⓐ Did you send a fax to the wrong place?

Ⓑ I'm sorry, I was blanking out.

---

2 ★ めがねがないと、**ぼうっと**して何も見えないんです。

★ *Megane ga nai to, bōtto shite nani mo mienai n desu.*

★ Without my glasses, I can't see anything clearly.

19

ぼんやり

Bon-yari

Vaguely

何(なに)かに気(き)を取(と)られて集中(しゅうちゅう)できない状態(じょうたい)、はっきりしない状態(じょうたい)。

To be distracted by something and unable to focus, or for things to not be clear.

ぼんやりする、ぼんやりしたN、ぼんやりとV

Point 見(み)ているものや考(かんが)えがはっきりしないこと。

For something being looked at or thought about to be unclear.

---

1 Ⓐ あの日(ひ)はその後(あと)、どこに行(い)きましたか。

Ⓑ さあ。記憶(きおく)が**ぼんやり**してしまって思(おも)い出(だ)せないんです。

Ⓐ *Ano hi wa sono ato, doko ni ikimashita ka?*

Ⓑ *Sā. Kioku ga bon-yari shite shimatte omoidasenai n desu.*

Ⓐ Where did you go that day after that?

Ⓑ Who knows. My memories are vague and I can't remember.

---

2 Ⓐ なに、**ぼんやり**してるんだよ。

Ⓑ ごめん。

Ⓐ *Nani, bon-yari shiteru n dayo.*

Ⓑ *Gomen.*

Ⓐ What are you acting so vaguely for?

Ⓑ Sorry.

20 うとうと

73

Nod off

Utouto

眠るつもりはないのに、眠くなって、一時的に眠ってしまう様子。

To get sleepy despite not intending to sleep and to sleep temporarily.

うとうとする、うとうとV「居眠りをする」、**うとうととV**

Point 居眠りをするときに使う。

Used when dozing off.

---

1 Ⓐ 田中さん、起きてください。着きましたよ。

Ⓑ あ、すみません。つい**ウトウト**してしまって。

Ⓐ *Tanaka san, okite kudasai. Tsukimashita yo.*

Ⓑ *A, sumimasen. Tsui utouto shite shimatte.*

Ⓐ Tanaka-san, please wake up. We're here.

Ⓑ Oh, sorry. I just happened to nod off.

---

2 ★ ここは暖かくて気持ちがいいから、**ウトウト**している人が多い。

★ *Koko wa atatakakute kimochi ga ī kara, utouto shiteiru hito ga ōi.*

★ It's warm and comfortable here, so there are a lot of people nodding off.

21

うっとり

Uttori

Rapt

美しいものや素晴らしいものに心を引かれている状態。

To be distracted by something beautiful or wonderful.

うっとりする、うっとりとV

Point 心を奪われ、夢を見ているような気分。

For one's heart to be stolen away and to feel like one is in a dream.

---

1 Ⓐ ピアノ、すごくよかったね。
Ⓑ うん。**うっとり**しちゃったよ。

Ⓐ *Piano, sugoku yokatta ne.*
Ⓑ *Un. Uttori shichatta yo.*

Ⓐ That piano was incredible.
Ⓑ Yes. I was rapt by it.

---

2 Ⓐ ずっと**うっとり**した目で見てたね。
Ⓑ すてきな指輪だなあって思って。

Ⓐ *Zutto uttori shita me de miteta ne.*
Ⓑ *Suteki na yubiwa danā tte omotte.*

Ⓐ You looked completely rapt the whole time.
Ⓑ I thought it was a wonderful ring.

22

うっかり

Ukkari

Absentmindedly

不注意で気づかない様子。

To be lax and not notice something.

うっかりする、うっかりV「忘れる」「間違える」、うっかりとV

Point するべきことをできなかったミスについて言うことが多い。

Often used to talk about a mistake made when something should have been done that was not.

---

1 Ⓐ すみません、今日は休みなんですが。 Ⓑ あっ、**うっかり**して曜日を間違えました。

Ⓐ *Sumimasen, kyō wa yasumi nan desu ga.*
Ⓑ *Att, ukkari shite yōbi o machigaemashita.*

Ⓐ Sorry, but today is a day off.
Ⓑ Oh, I absentmindedly got the day wrong.

---

2 ★ **うっかり**して目覚ましをかけるのを忘れちゃった。

★ *Ukkari shite mezamashi o kakeru no o wasure chatta.*

★ I absentmindedly forgot to set an alarm.

驚き(おどろ) Surprise

23 びっくり Bikkuri

74

突然(とつぜん)、予想(よそう)しないことが起(お)きて、驚(おどろ)く様子(ようす)。
For something unexpected to happen suddenly and to be surprised.

びっくりする、びっくりだ、びっくりとV

Point 驚(おどろ)いたことを表(あらわ)すとき、会話(かいわ)でいちばんよく使(つか)われる。
Most often used in conversations to express surprise.

1 Ⓐ 鈴木(すずき)さん!!
Ⓑ わっ、**びっくり**した！　こんなところで会(あ)うなんて。

Ⓐ *Suzuki san!!*
Ⓑ *Watt, bikkuri shita! Konna tokoro de au nante.*

Ⓐ Suzuki-san!!
Ⓑ Ah, you surprised me! I can't believe I met you in a place like this.

2 ★ 5月(がつ)に雪(ゆき)が降(ふ)るなんて、**びっくり**です。

★ *Go gatsu ni yuki ga furu nante, bikkuri desu.*

★ For something unexpected to happen suddenly and to be surprised.

24

ドッキリ／ドキッ

Dokkiri/ Dokitt

Startling

突然のことに、心臓が止まるように感じるほど驚く様子。

For something to happen suddenly to the point that it feels as though one's heart might stop.

ドッキリする、ドキッとV

Point 心臓が一瞬止まるイメージ。

Conjures the image of a heart stopping for a moment.

---

1 Ⓐ あー、**ドッキリ**した。びっくりさせないでよ。

Ⓑ ごめん、ごめん。

Ⓐ *Ā, dokkiri shita. Bikkuri sasenaide yo.*

Ⓑ *Gomen, gomen.*

Ⓐ Oh, you startled me. Don't surprise me like that.

Ⓑ Sorry, sorry.

---

2 ★ 知らない人に突然、名前を呼ばれて、**ドキッと**した。

★ *Shiranai hito ni totsuzen, namae o yobarete, dokitto shita.*

★ Someone I don't know suddenly calling my name startled me.

我慢(がまん)の限界(げんかい) The limit of one's patience

25 (75)

イライラ

Iraira

Irritated

思(おも)い通(どお)りにならず、焦(あせ)ったり、怒(おこ)りやすくなったりする様子(ようす)。
For things to go not as expected and to feel easily anxious or angry.

イライライする、イライラとV

Point 待(ま)っているものがなかなか来(こ)ない場面(ばめん)でよく使(つか)う。
Often used in situations where something awaited is not coming.

---

1 Ⓐ 今日(きょう)は彼女(かのじょ)のそばに行(い)かないほうがいいよ。
Ⓑ そうだね。ずっと**イライラ**してるものね。

Ⓐ *Kyō wa kanojo no soba ni ikanai hō ga ī yo.*
Ⓑ *Sō da ne. Zutto iraira shiteru mono ne.*

Ⓐ You should probably not go near her today.
Ⓑ You're right. She's been irritated for a long time.

---

2 ★ バスが全然(ぜんぜん)来(こ)なくて、**イライラ**した。

★ *Basu ga zenzen konakute, iraira shita.*

★ I was irritated that the bus didn't come at all.

26

イラッと

Iratto

瞬間的(しゅんかんてき)にイライラする様子(ようす)。

To be momentarily annoyed.

Typical forms イラっとする、イラっとV「来(く)る」

Point 人(ひと)の言葉(ことば)や態度(たいど)に対(たい)してよく使(つか)う。

Often used regarding a person's words or actions.

1

Ⓐ あの言(い)い方(かた)、**イラッと**するよ。
Ⓑ わかる。

Ⓐ *Ano ī kata, iratto suru yo.*
Ⓑ *Wakaru.*

Ⓐ The way they say that ticks me off.
Ⓑ I know what you mean.

2

★ 最近(さいきん)の学生(がくせい)ってマナー知(し)らなくて、**イラッと**来(く)るね。

★ *Saikin no gakusē tte manā shiranakute, iratto kuru ne.*

★ Students lately don't know their manners and it ticks me off.

27

76

ピリピリ

Piripiri

Prickly

緊張(きんちょう)が高(たか)まって、神経質(しんけいしつ)になる様子(ようす)。

To be very tense to the point of feeling nervous.

ピリピリする、ピリピリとV

Point ちょっとしたことに敏感(びんかん)に反応(はんのう)する状態(じょうたい)。

To react sensitively to something minor.

---

1 Ⓐ まあまあ、そんなに**ピリピリ**しないで。

Ⓑ 無理(むり)だよ。試験(しけん)は明日(あした)なんだから。

Ⓐ *Māmā, sonna ni piripiri shinaide.*

Ⓑ *Muri dayo. Shiken wa ashita nan da kara.*

Ⓐ Now, now. Don't be so prickly.

Ⓑ I can't help it. The test is tomorrow.

---

2 ★ 店長(てんちょう)はいつも**ピリピリ**しているから、アルバイトは大変(たいへん)だよ。

★ *Tenchō wa itsumo piripiri shite iru kara arubaito wa taihen da yo.*

★ The manager is always acting prickly, so the part-timers have a tough time.

28

うんざり

Unzari

Disgusted

何かに飽きたりあきれたりして、もういやだと思う様子。

To feel tired and appalled by something to the point of not wanting to deal with it anymore.

うんざりする、うんざりだ、うんざりとV

Point これ以上、もうがまんできない、という気持ち。

The feeling of not being able to take something any more.

1

Ⓐ もう、こんな仕事、**うんざり**。早くやめたいよ。

Ⓑ 大変そうだね。

Ⓐ *Mō, konna shigoto, unzari. Hayaku yametai yo.*

Ⓑ *Taihen sō da ne.*

Ⓐ I'm disgusted by this job. I want to hurry up and quit.

Ⓑ It seems tough.

2

★ 彼女、人の悪口ばかりで、**うんざり**する。

★ *Kanojo, hito no waruguchi bakari de, unzari suru.*

★ She always badmouths people, I'm disgusted by it.

混乱 Confusion

29

77

あたふた

Panicked

Atafuta

ひどくあわてて、全く普通の状態でいられない様子。

To be incredibly flustered to the point of being completely unable to act normally.

あたふたする、あたふたとV

Point 急に時間がない状況になったときなどによく使う。

Often used when in a situation where there is suddenly no more time.

---

1 Ⓐ あれもこれもしなければならなくて、**あたふた**しています。

Ⓑ 大変ですね。

Ⓐ *Are mo kore mo shinakereba naranakute, atafuta shite imasu.*

Ⓑ *Taihen desu ne.*

Ⓐ I was panicked since I had to do this and that.

Ⓑ That must be tough.

---

2 Ⓐ 田中さんは？

Ⓑ 社長に急に呼ばれて、**あたふた**と出て行きました。

Ⓐ *Tanaka san wa?*

Ⓑ *Shachō ni kyū ni yobarete, atafuta to dete ikimashita.*

Ⓐ What about Tanaka-san?

Ⓑ He was suddenly called in by the president and went in a panic.

30

オロオロ

Orooro

Flustered

どうしていいかわからず、落(お)ち着(つ)かない様子(ようす)。

To be unsure of what to do and to be unstable.

オロオロする、オロオロとV

Point 問題(もんだい)の解決方法(かいけつほうほう)がわからず、ちょっとしたパニックになっている。

To be slightly panicked, not knowing how to solve a problem.

---

1 Ⓐ 何(なに)もわからなくて、**オロオロ**するばかりです。

Ⓑ 大丈夫(だいじょうぶ)ですよ。みんな手伝(てつだ)いますから。

Ⓐ *Nani mo wakaranakute, orooro suru bakari desu.*

Ⓑ *Daijōbu desu yo. Minna tetsudaimasu kara.*

Ⓐ I don't know anything and so I'm nothing but flustered.

Ⓑ It's okay. Everyone will help you out.

---

2 ★ **オロオロ**する必要(ひつよう)はないよ。自信(じしん)持(も)って。

★ *Orooro suru hitsuyō wa nai yo. Jishin motte.*

★ There's no reason to be flustered. Be confident.

後悔(こうかい)・不満(ふまん) Regret / Dissatisfaction

31

もやもや

Moyamoya

Uncertainty

心(こころ)に引(ひ)っかかることがあり、すっきりしない心(こころ)の状態(じょうたい)。

To not feel refreshed because something is lingering in one's heart.

もやもやする、もやもやとV

Point 「もや」はうすい霧(きり)。心(こころ)が晴(は)れない状態(じょうたい)。

「もや」means thin fog. For one's heart to stay unclear.

---

1 Ⓐ なんか、**もやもや**するんだよね。
Ⓑ まあ、気持(きも)ちはわかるけど。

Ⓐ *Nanka, moyamoya suru n da yo ne.*
Ⓑ *Mā, kimochi wa wakaru kedo.*

Ⓐ I feel uncertain for some reason.
Ⓑ Well, I understand how you feel.

---

2 ★ 気分(きぶん)が**もやもや**するときは、音楽(おんがく)を聴(き)くようにしています。

★ *Kibun ga moyamoya suru toki wa, ongaku o kiku yō ni shite imasu.*

★ I listen to music whenever I feel uncertain.

32

くよくよ

Brooding

Kuyokuyo

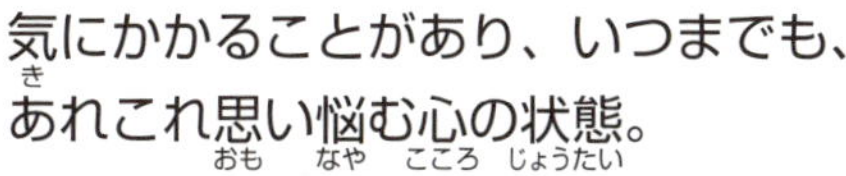
気にかかることがあり、いつまでも、あれこれ思い悩む心の状態。

To be constantly worrying over something concerning.

Typical forms **くよくよする、くよくよとV**

Point 済んだことをいつまでも気にすることについて言う。

Used when talking about something that one continues to worry about despite being over.

---

1 Ⓐ いつまでも、**くよくよ**しないほうがいいよ。
Ⓑ ありがとう。

Ⓐ *Itsumademo, kuyokuyo shinai hō ga ī yo.*
Ⓑ *Arigatō.*

Ⓐ You shouldn't be brooding over it forever.
Ⓑ Thanks.

---

2 Ⓐ そんなことで、**くよくよ**することないよ。
Ⓑ うん、わかってる。

Ⓐ *Sonna koto de, kuyokuyo suru koto nai yo.*
Ⓑ *Un,wakatteru.*

Ⓐ That's nothing to brood over.
Ⓑ Yes, thanks.

心の変化　An emotional change

33

79

ホッと

Hotto

Relieved

緊張や不安、心配がなくなって、安心した状態。

For the worry regarding nervousness or anxiety to go away, feeling relieved.

ホッとする

Point 緊張がなくなり、大きく息をするイメージ。

Conjures the image of taking a deep breath after no longer feeling stressed.

---

1 Ⓐ 全員無事だと聞いて、**ホッと**しました。
Ⓑ ご心配をおかけしました。

Ⓐ *Zen-in buji da to kīte, hotto shimashita.*
Ⓑ *Go shinpai o okake shimashita.*

Ⓐ When I heard everyone was okay, I was relieved.
Ⓑ I'm sorry to have worried you.

---

2 ★ やっぱり、うちに帰ると**ホッと**します。

★ *Yappari, uchi ni kaeru to hotto shimasu.*

★ After all, coming home makes me feel relieved.

34

スッと →p.48

Sutto

Refreshingly

心配や不満、疑問などがなくなり、気持ちが晴れる様子。

For one's worries or unease to suddenly disappear, causing one's feelings to become clear.

スッとする

Point 不快に思っていたものがなくなり、気分がよくなったときに使う。

Used when feeling better after something thought of as unpleasant goes away.

---

1 Ⓐ 手続きは時間かかりましたか。
Ⓑ いえ。問題なく、**スッと**できました。

Ⓐ *Tetsuzuki wa jikan kakarimashita ka?*
Ⓑ *Ie. Mondai naku, sutto dekimashita.*

Ⓐ Did the procedures take time?
Ⓑ No. There was no problem and it went refreshingly.

---

2 Ⓐ パソコン、直った？
Ⓑ やっとね。原因がわかって、**スッと**したよ。

Ⓐ *Pasokon, naotta?*
Ⓑ *Yatto ne. Gen-in ga wakatte, sutto shita yo.*

Ⓐ Did the computer get better?
Ⓑ Finally, yes. We figured out the problem and things were refreshed.

35

80

ハッと
Hatto

Startled

急に思い出したり気づいたりする様子。
To suddenly remember or notice something.

ハッとする

Point 予期していなかったことがきっかけになることが多い。
Often used when the cause is something unexpected.

1 Ⓐ 先生の言葉にハッとしました。私が悪かったんです。
Ⓑ そうですか。

Ⓐ *Sensē no kotoba ni hatto shimashita. Watashi ga warukatta n desu.*
Ⓑ *Sō desu ka.*

Ⓐ Sensei's words startled me. I was in the wrong.
Ⓑ Is that so.

2 ★ ハッと気づいたことをメモするようにしています。

★ *Hatto kizuita koto o memo suru yō ni shite imasu.*

★ I note down the things that I noticed when startled.

36

ふと
Futo

Suddenly

特(とく)に理由(りゆう)や意識(いしき)をすることなく、突然(とつぜん)に。

For something to happen all of a sudden, without any particular reason or intention.

Typical forms ふとV「思(おも)い出(だ)す」「気(き)になる」

Point 特(とく)に理由(りゆう)もなく、なんとなく、という場合(ばあい)に使(つか)う。

Used in situations where something just happens for no particular reason.

---

1 Ⓐ **ふと**思(おも)い出(だ)したんだけど、トムはどうしてるかなあ。

Ⓑ そうだね、どうしてるかな。

Ⓐ *Futo omoidashita n dakedo, Tomu wa dō shiteru kanā.*

Ⓑ *Sō dane, dō shiteru kana.*

Ⓐ I suddenly remembered, but what is Tom doing now?

Ⓑ You're right, I wonder what he's doing.

---

2 ★ あの小(ちい)さな本屋(ほんや)がどうなったか、**ふと**気(き)になったんです。

★ *Ano chīsana hon-ya ga dō natta ka, futo ki ni natta n desu.*

★ I suddenly wondered what that small bookstore was doing.

37

81

ゾッと

Zotto

Shiver

恐ろしさにふるえたり寒気がしたりする様子。

To feel cold because of a chilling fear.

ゾッとする

Point 「ぞっ」は体がふるえる様子。

「ぞっ」is the image of a shaking body.

---

1 Ⓐ ひろし君、危なかったですね。
Ⓑ ええ。思い出すだけでゾッとします。

Ⓐ *Hiroshi kun, abunakatta desu ne.*
Ⓑ *Ē. Omoidasu dake de zotto shimasu.*

Ⓐ That was close for Hiroshi-kun.
Ⓑ Yes. Just thinking about it makes me shiver.

---

2 Ⓐ 部長と二人で出張に行くかもしれないの？
Ⓑ 私と部長で？　やめてよ、ゾッとする。

Ⓐ *Buchō to futari de shucchō ni iku kamo shirenai no?*
Ⓑ *Watashi to buchō de? Yamete yo, zotto suru.*

Ⓐ So you might go together alone with the division chief?
Ⓑ Me and him? Stop it, that gives me the shivers.

38

ピンと

Pinto

To understand suddenly

瞬間的に、そう感じた様子、自分の気持ちに訴えるものがあると感じた様子。

To feel a certain way in a moment, or to feel something that appeals to one's feelings.

ピンと来る

Point 「ピン」で「直感ですぐそれと感じる」イメージを表している。

「ピン」is used to create the image of something being felt directly and immediately.

---

1 Ⓐ あの人が犯人だと**ピンと**来ました。
Ⓑ そうなんですか。

Ⓐ It suddenly came to me that he was the culprit.
Ⓑ Is that so?

Ⓐ *Ano hito ga hannin da to pinto kimashita.*
Ⓑ *Sō nan desu ka.*

---

2 ★ この壁の色、なんか**ピンと**来ないんだよなあ。

★ The color of that sky doesn't come to me exactly.

★ *Kono kabe no iro, nanka pinto konai n da yo nā.*

気分 Feeling

39 

さっぱり

→p. 155

Cleanly

Sappari

不快さや引っかかるところがなく、気持ちのよい様子。

To feel good, without any unease or hitches.

 Typical forms **さっぱりする、さっぱりVない**「わからない」、**さっぱりとV**

Point 不快なもの、心に引っかかるものがなくなったときの気分。

The feeling of something unpleasant or nagging going away.

---

1 Ⓐ スポーツやっている人って、**さっぱり**している人が多いね。
Ⓑ そうかも。

Ⓐ *Supōtsu yatte iru hito tte, sappari shite iru hito ga ōi ne.*
Ⓑ *Sō kamo.*

Ⓐ There are a lot of clean people who play sports.
Ⓑ You might be right.

---

2 ★ やっと、この会社をやめられると思うと、気分が**さっぱり**する。

★ *Yatto, kono kaisha o yamerareru to omou to, kibun ga sappari suru.*

★ Finally, my heart feels clean thinking that I can quite this company next year.

40

すっきり →p. 154

Sukkiri

Refreshed

余計なものや面倒なものがなく、気持ちがよい様子。

To feel good, not worrying about anything extraneous or annoying.

すっきりV「する」、**すっきりとV**

Point 余計なもの、はっきりしないものがなくなったときの気分。

The feeling of something unnecessary or undecided going away.

---

1 Ⓐ どう？ 少しは気分落ち着いた？
Ⓑ はい、おかげさまで。だいぶ**すっきり**しました。

Ⓐ So? Feel a little calmer?
Ⓑ Yes, thanks you to. I feel much more refreshed.

Ⓐ *Dō? Sukoshi wa kibun ochitsuita?*
Ⓑ *Hai, okagesama de. Daibu sukkiri shimashita.*

---

2 ★ 言いたいことを言ったら、気持ちが**すっきり**しました。

★ I felt very refreshed when I said what I wanted to say.

★ *Ītai koto o ittara, kimochi ga sukkiri shimashita.*

怒り Anger

41

カッと

Katto

To flare up

瞬間的に怒り、興奮する様子。

To be momentarily angry, to become excited

カッとする／カッとなる

Point 瞬間的に頭に血が上るイメージ。

Conjures the image of blood suddenly rising to the head.

---

1 Ⓐ すみません、つい**カッと**なってしまって。
Ⓑ いいんです。大丈夫です。

Ⓐ *Sumimasen, tsui katto natte shimatte.*
Ⓑ *Ī n desu. Daijōbu desu.*

Ⓐ Sorry, I flared up there.
Ⓑ It's okay. It's fine.

---

2 ★ 先に**カッと**なったほうが、負けだよ。

★ *Saki ni katto natta hō ga, make da yo.*

★ Whoever flares up first loses.

42

カチンと

Kachinto

To be offended

気持ちを傷つけるようなことに、怒りを感じる様子。

To feel anger due to something that hurts one's feelings.

Typical forms カチンとV「来る」

Point 誰かの一言が非常に不愉快だったときによく使う。

Often used when someone's words are extremely unpleasant.

1

Ⓐ どうして、そう**カチンと**来ることばかり言うんだ？
Ⓑ あなただって、そうじゃない。

Ⓐ *Dōshite, sō kachin to kuru koto bakari iu n da?*
Ⓑ *Anata datte , sō ja nai.*

Ⓐ Why do you always say those kinds of offensive things?
Ⓑ You're the same, you know.

2

★ 彼の言い方に**カチンと**来てしまい、連絡をとっていません。

★ *Kare no īkata ni kachin to kite shimai, renraku o totte imasen.*

★ I got offended by what he said, so I haven't contacted him.

43

84

ムッと

Mutto

Miffed

怒って、表情が固くなってしまう様子。

To be angry and for one's expression to freeze.

ムッとする、ムッとV「来る」

Point 外に出さないようにしながらも、怒りで表情が変わる様子を表す。

When one's expression changes due to anger despite trying to hold it in.

---

1 Ⓐ そんなに**ムッと**しないでよ。
Ⓑ そうなるようなことを言うからでしょ。

Ⓐ *Sonna ni mutto shinaide yo.*
Ⓑ *Sō naru yōna koto o iu kara desho.*

Ⓐ Don't act so miffed.
Ⓑ It's because you said something that makes me do this.

---

2 ★ あんな態度じゃ、**ムッと**されても仕方ないよね。

★ *Anna taido ja, mutto saretemo shikata nai yo ne.*

★ You can't blame someone for being miffed if you act that way.

44

ムカムカ →p.144

Offended

Mukamuka

心の底から怒りがわいて来る様子。

To be angry from the bottom of one's heart.

Typical forms **ムカムカする、ムカムカとV**

Point 急に怒りの感情がわいてくること。

For one's anger to suddenly boil up.

---

1 Ⓐ あいつの顔を見ているだけで**ムカムカ**する。
Ⓑ まあまあ、そう言わないで。

Ⓐ *Aitsu no kao o miteiru dake de mukamuka suru.*
Ⓑ *Māmā, sō iwanaide.*

Ⓐ I feel offended just looking at his face.
Ⓑ Now, now. Don't way that.

---

2 ★ 思い出したら、また**ムカムカ**してきた。

★ *Omoidashitara, mata mukamuka shite kita.*

★ Thinking of it makes me offended again.

45

カンカン

Kankan

Furious

怒りが瞬間的に最高に達している様子。

For one's anger to momentarily reach a peak.

カンカンにV 「怒る」「なる」、**カンカンとV**

Point 瞬間的な怒りがMAXになっているときに使う。

Used when one's anger momentarily reaches a maximum.

---

1 Ⓐ 早く行った方がいいよ。石川さん、**カンカン**に怒ってたから。

Ⓑ わかった。ありがとう。

Ⓐ *Hayaku itta hō ga ī yo. Ishikawa san, kankan ni okotteta kara.*

Ⓑ *Wakatta. Arigatō.*

Ⓐ You should hurry up and say that. Ishikawa-san was furious.

Ⓑ Okay. Thanks.

---

2 ★ そんなことをしたら、社長、**カンカン**になると思うよ。

★ *Sonna koto o shitara, shachō, kankan ni naru to omou yo.*

★ I think that the president will be furious if you do that.

英語さくいん

Index (English version)

*Alphabetical order

O

P

Q

R

S

日本語さくいん
Index (Japanese version)

*Alphabetical order

A

B

C

D

F

G

How to Download Voice Data

STEP 1

Access the voice download website!	(Input the following URL:) **URL : http://audiobook.jp/exchange/jresearch**

STEP 2

Continue to "audiobook.jp" registration page from the one displayed to register as a member.	Click「audiobook.jp に会員登録(無料)」(Register to be a Memberof the "audiobook.jp" (Free)) ※ To download voice data, you must register for the "audiobook.jp"(registration is free). Enter your email address, password (8 or more alphanumeric characters), name, birthday, and gender on the registration page ▶ Read the Terms of Service ▶ Click「確認」(Confirm) ▶ Registration complete

STEP 3

Return to the download page from the「ご登録が完了しました」page.	Click「ダウンロードページ」(Download Page), then enter "23874" in the field under「シリアルコードをご入力ください」(Please enter your serial code) on the page displayed and click「送信」(Send).

STEP 4

Download voice data.	Click「無料でオーディオブックを受け取る」▶ Click「本棚で確認する」▶ Click「ダウンロード」(Download「全体版」) ※ If you are using a PC, please download voice data from「本棚」. If you are using a smartphone, a guide will appear for the app. Please use the voice files through the app.

Notice

- Voice data can be played from your PC, your iPhone, or your Android smartphone.
- Voice data can be downloaded and played as many times as you wish.
- For questions about downloads, please contact: info@febe.jp (Emails will be received from 10 AM to 8 PM on weekdays).

音声ダウンロードの手順

STEP 1

音声ダウンロード用のサイトにアクセス！	（下記 URL を直接入力） **URL：http://audiobook.jp/exchange/jresearch**

STEP 2

表示されたページから、audiobook.jp への登録ページに進み、会員登録をする。	「audiobook.jpに会員登録（無料）」をクリック ※ 音声のダウンロードには、audiobook.jp への会員登録（無料）が必要です。 登録ページでメールアドレス・パスワード（英数字の８ケタ以上）・名前・生年月日・性別を入力 ▶ 規約を読む ▶「確認」をクリック ▶ 登録完了

STEP 3

「ご登録が完了しました」のページからダウンロードのページに戻る。	「ダウンロードページ」をクリックして、表示されたページの「シリアルコードをご入力ください」の下の欄に「23874」を入力して「送信」をクリックする。

STEP 4

音声をダウンロードする。	「無料でオーディオブックを受け取る」をクリック ▶「本棚で確認する」をクリック ▶「ダウンロード」をクリック（「全体版」をダウンロード） ※ PC の場合は、「本棚」から音声をダウンロードしてください。スマートフォンの場合は、アプリの案内が出ますので、アプリからご利用ください。

ご注意

- PC からでも、iPhone や Android のスマートフォンからでも音声を再生いただけます。
- 音声は何度でもダウンロード・再生いただくことができます。
- ダウンロードについてのお問い合わせ先：info@febe.jp（受付時間：平日の 10～20時）

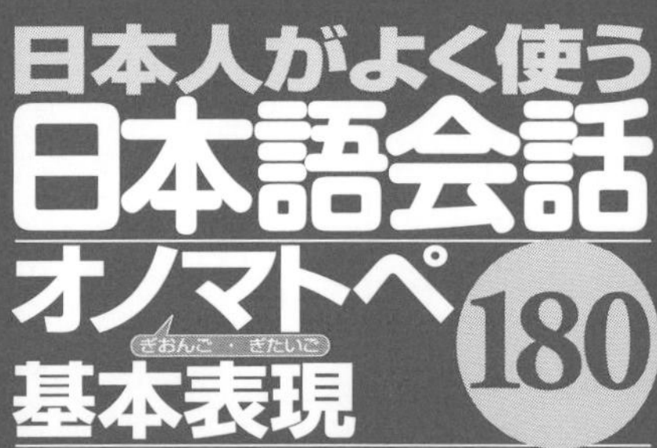

180 Basic Onomatopoeia (Giongo-Gitaigo) Expressions Used by Native Japanese Speakers in Regular Conversation

ISBN978-4-86392-387-4

ISBN978-4-86392-387-4
C2081 ¥1600E

9784863923874

1922081016000

定価（本体1600円+税）

Jリサーチ出版

180 Basic Onomatopoeia (Giongo-Gitaigo)
Expressions Used by Native Japanese Speakers
in Regular Conversation